WHY YOU FEEL THE WAY YOU DO

Understand and Heal the Source
of Stressful Emotions

"*Why You Feel the Way You Do* is a must read for those wanting to better understand the complexities of personality and choice. . . Peurifoy does a masterful job of bringing research and personal wisdom into helping us have more grace as we master the art of loving ourselves."

SARAH K. RAMSEY, Author of *Problem Solved: Simple Habits for Complex Decisions* and *Becoming Toxic Person Proof*

"There are times in life where you receive validation of the core principles you live by and diligently work on to get better as a person. *Why You Feel the Way You Do* does that for me. Without emotional control, it is impossible to achieve long-term success. Thus, no matter what you've been through, there are no excuses, especially if you hold this book in your hands. Salute!"

DC GLENN, Actor, Voice Artist, Speaker, Multi-Platinum Artist of the Rap Group Tag Team. Creator of *Whoomp!* and *Scoop! There it is.* (GEICO)

"*Why You Feel the Way You Do* gives you insight into your emotions and helps you decipher them."

ELAINE LALANNE, Co-Author of *If You Want to Live, Move: Putting The Boom Back into Boomers*

"Reneau has written an informative and helpful book. He not only provides readers with an understanding of why our difficult feelings arise, but specific actions readers can take to transform them into more positive and healthy patterns of thinking and acting."

LORI COVINGTON, M.A., MBACP, Author of *10 Cures for Loneliness*

Why You Feel the Way You Do

Understand and Heal the Source of Stressful Emotions

RENEAU Z. PEURIFOY

DeVorss **⊘** Publications
Camarillo, California

ISBN Print Edition: 978-0-87516-931-6
eBook ISBN: 978-087516-932-3

Library of Congress Control Number: 2022046445

First DeVorss Publications Edition, 2023

Printed in The United States of America
DeVorss & Company, Publishers
PO Box 1389
Camarillo CA 93011-1389
www.devorss.com

Names: Peurifoy, Reneau Z., author.
Title: Why you feel the way you do / by Reneau Z. Peurifoy, MA.
Description: First DeVorss Publications edition. | Camarillo, California: DeVorss Publications, 2023. | Summary:
"Emotions have been affecting people since the beginning of time, as well as our never-ending need to understand them. WHY YOU FEEL THE WAY YOU DO is different in that it approaches emotions using the insights that have emerged from the relatively new field of neuroscience. This timely and informative book starts by explaining what neuroscience has discovered about emotions. It then uses this information to show how common problems with emotions emerge along with ways to heal them. Of particular help is the concept called 'core beliefs' that helps the reader identify fundamental patterns. Of special interest, this book looks at the destructive emotions of guilt and shame along with ways to manage them, and how social media and electronic devices can affect emotional development." –Provided by publisher.
Identifiers: LCCN 2022046445 (print) | LCCN 2022046446 (ebook) | ISBN 9780875169316 (trade paperback) | ISBN 9780875169323 (ebook)

Subjects: LCSH: Emotions – Psychological aspects. | Human behavior. | Neurosciences.
Classification: LCC BF511.P48 2023 (print) | LCC BF511 (ebook)
DDC 152.4—dc23/eng/20221213
LC record available at https://lccn.loc.gov/2022046445
LC ebook record available at https://lccn.loc.gov/2022046446

Author's Note

The ideas, procedures, and suggestions in this book are not intended as a substitute for consulting with either a physician or a psychotherapist. You should regularly consult a physician in matters relating to your health, particularly with respect to any symptoms that may require diagnosis or medical attention. Likewise, if you are finding it difficult to cope with daily life or stressful events, you are urged to seek help from a qualified psychotherapist.

Acknowledgments

This idea for this book began when Danielle Seadia, an associate who I had lost contact with, reached out and asked me to write a book on emotions for the general public. She served as my book agent and arranged its publication with Gary Peattie, the publisher at DeVorss & Company. Thank you for the opportunity.

My wife, Michiyo, patiently read the rough drafts and pointed out areas in need of further work. I then sent the revisions to Vallin Bingley for initial proofing. Next, they went to Stephanie Francis, Ana Hantt, and Josie Baron who provided insightful comments that improved both the content and readability of each chapter. Jacquelyn Neal, was the final reader before sending it to the publisher. Marta M. Mobley was the editor for DeVorss & Company. She did an excellent job of catching errors and offering suggestions to make the final manuscript more readable.

As with any book of this type, it's important to acknowledge the countless researchers and therapists seeking a better understanding of emotions. I not only stand on their shoulders, but I am also deeply indebted to the hundreds of people struggling with difficult emotions who shared their lives with me. Thank you for the insights you have given to me.

Contents

Introduction

I grew up in a home filled with many different types of animals. In addition to a dog and cat, we had a parrot, rabbits, and chickens. Our parrot, Greeny, was my favorite. He would sit on a perch in the middle of the table when we ate breakfast and sometimes at other meals. It became his routine to leave his perch and walk over to one of our plates to sneak a piece of food that he liked, then return to his perch. Or sometimes after eating his food, he enjoyed sitting on my leg and having his head rubbed on a small bald spot.

Interacting with all these animals gave me a keen interest in animal behavior. This interest was sharpened in high school when I read about the work of Konrad Lorenz, one of the founding fathers of the field of ethology, the study of animal behavior. It fascinated me to learn how the birds Lorenz studied formed an immediate bond between a newly hatched bird and its caregiver, which he termed, imprinting.

While majoring in biology at university, my main interest was always animal behavior. After graduating, I earned a secondary teaching credential and taught for five years.

During this period, I had a good friend, Tim, who was a counselor. Listening to his experiences convinced me that I had found my calling. While earning my master's degree in counseling, I found cognitive behavioral psychology the most appealing of the various types of therapy I studied. The idea that you can change many types of dysfunctional behaviors by changing how you think and practicing new behaviors matched my previous interest in animal behavior.

As I began working in the field of anxiety disorders, I found the cognitive behavioral approach worked well. However, there were times when something more was needed with deeply ingrained emotional responses. Because of this, I trained in additional approaches such as hypnotherapy, neurolinguistic programing (NLP) and eye movement desensitization and reprocessing (EMDR).

Writing this book gave me the opportunity to delve into the new discoveries that have been made in the field of affective neuroscience, the study of the neural mechanisms of emotion. These findings not only provide a clearer understanding of why we have emotions, and how they work, but also reveal the deep connection we have with all other mammals—something every pet owner understands.

In writing this book, I decided to structure it in the form of a narrative arc that would begin with a brief overview of how emotions are generated by these circuits deep in the brain. It then uses this research as a springboard for the main sections of the book that deal with the various types of difficult emotional reactions that everyone experiences from time to time. And the final section describes what the emerging field of positive psychology has discovered. This area of research focuses on well-being, success, and high-functioning individuals. The popular press often refers to this as "the science of happiness."

My work as a clinician helping people struggling with difficult emotions provides an important inspiration for my writing. I always want to go beyond simply providing interesting information and include practical tools that readers can use to live more successful and happy lives. Because of this, I include a section titled, "Things to Do" at the end of each chapter. The activities in this section come from my years of both reading about emotions and working as a therapist.

Even if you are only reading this book to gain new information, I encourage you to do the activities as they provide practical ways to hear more clearly the messages that your emotions are telling you, and provide tools for managing emotions that may have been difficult to experience or may have caused you to do things you later regretted.

As you read through the chapters, you'll find that some activities are easy, while others are more challenging and may even make you uncomfortable. Those that you find to be easy, probably deal with skills that are already part of how you manage emotions. Those you find difficult or uncomfortable will most likely involve skills and ideas that are new to you or that you are still learning to master. Either way, I think you'll find taking time to work through them well worth the effort.

Because this book is intended for a general audience, I have kept footnotes to a minimum and only included them when a term might be new to the reader. If you wish to learn more about any of the people or areas of research mentioned, a search on the Internet will provide a wealth of information. Now, let the journey begin!

Chapter 1:

The Seven Core Emotional Systems

We hate and we love, can one tell me why?
– Catullus (84-54 BC)

Emotions are such an essential part of who you are. Indeed, life would be empty and meaningless without them. Love, joy, and the excitement of new discoveries can make life a wonderful experience. At the same time, fear, anger, and sadness can intrude into your life and produce misery beyond what words can express.

This chapter lays the foundation for understanding why we have emotions. This understanding is built upon in later chapters that show you how to manage them more effectively. It starts with a look at what science has learned about emotions over the past hundred years. Then, it describes the seven basic emotions humans share with all other mammals, the circuits that generate these emotions, and how these circuits come to be activated and regulated by the thinking part of the brain[1].

---

[1] The "thinking part of the brain" refers to the cerebral cortex. The emotional systems discussed in this chapter are in the subcortex which is located below the cerebral cortex and is completely covered by it.

AFFECTS

While love, sadness, anger, pity, and fear have been written about for thousands of years, they were not grouped together under a single psychology term until relatively recently. In 1859, the Scottish psychologist Alexander Bain used the word "emotion" to cover "all that is understood by feelings, states of feeling, pleasures, pains, passions, sentiments, and affections." This use of the word "emotion" began a fundamental shift in the vocabulary used to describe how the mind works. The only problem was that, for the next hundred years, there was no agreement on what emotions were and how they were triggered.

The word "emotion" itself is derived from the Latin verb "emovere" which means "to move out." And this is what emotions do: The word describes feelings that urge you to act in some way. For example, fear causes you to want to get away from whatever is causing you to be afraid.

Today, the field of neuroscience[2] uses the term "affect" to describe the various types of feelings and emotions you experience. Affects themselves are classified into three categories.

The first category includes sensory affects, such as the sweetness you experience when sugar is placed on the tongue or the experience of heat or cold. The second category is homeostatic affects[3]. These drive you to take the actions needed to satisfy the physical needs of your body, such as hunger and thirst that drive you to

---

[2] Neuroscience is the study of the human brain and nervous system.

[3] Homeostasis is used to refer to something that is in a state of balance, such as when the water and salt in your body are in proper proportion to each other. Homeostatic affects are feelings that urge you to do something to restore metabolic balance of some kind in your body, such as drinking water when you're dehydrated or eating when your body needs energy.

eat and drink water. The third category comprises your emotional affects—the ones this book is about.

Currently, neuroscience has identified seven core emotion systems in the brains of all mammals. Each system triggers the same behaviors in animals and humans. While there is no way of knowing what animals are experiencing, when these systems are triggered in you, they produce the feelings that we call emotions.

THE SEVEN EMOTIONAL SYSTEMS

The discovery of the brain's emotional systems began with Walter Hess. He was one of the first people to identify portions of the brain associated with a specific emotional effect. While experimenting with cats in the 1930s, he found he could trigger different behaviors by applying tiny electric impulses to different parts of the hypothalamus, an interior part of the brain. When he did this, cats would display defensive and aggressive behaviors or curl up and go to sleep, depending on the location that was being stimulated with the electrical impulse.

In the 1990s, Jaak Panksepp coined the term "affective neuroscience," which today is seen as a discipline that studies the brain mechanisms underlying emotions. Currently, seven emotional systems have been identified in the brains of humans and every other mammal that has been studied.

These seven emotional systems are foundational tools for living that are built into us at birth. For example, it is not necessary to teach babies or young animals to become angry, fearful, or to panic. At the same time, these systems are shaped by experience, and change as a person or animal learns how to adapt to life's challenges.

The systems that produce the various pleasurable feelings you experience include the SEEKING, LUST, CARE, and PLAY emotional systems. Along with these are three systems that produce unpleasant feelings: FEAR, RAGE, and PANIC. Neuroscientists capitalize each of these words to indicate that they are referring to primary emotional systems in the brain. This helps distinguish these terms from the way we usually use each word.

The SEEKING/Desire System is essential for all the other emotional systems to operate effectively. It generates an urge to explore and engage with the world with eager curiosity and interest. You see this in young mammals, such as kittens and puppies, as they explore and learn about their environment. You also see this in infants as they stare with fascination at their hands and learn to coordinate their bodies. Later, as they gain the ability to crawl and then walk, this system urges them to explore their world. The SEEKING system helps animals find and eagerly anticipate all kinds of resources needed for survival, such as water, food, and warmth. As an adult, this system helps you become absorbed in the things that interest you and explore new possibilities.

The PLAY/Physical Social-Engagement system urges both young children and young mammals to engage in physical play like wrestling, running, and chasing each other. This type of play helps them bond socially and learn social limits, what behaviors are permissible, and what behaviors are taboo. In humans, this carries over in the "ribbing" and joking that continues to add fun in adulthood as well as the many other forms of adult play. While the circuits identified with the PLAY system are in the inner part of the brain, brain imaging shows the outer portion of the brain where you do your thinking lights up during play. This corresponds with research which indicates that play enhances learning. It also shows that these circuits deep inside of your brain become tightly integrated with those in the outside, thinking portion.

The CARE/Maternal Nurturance system seems to be mostly found in mammals, and helps to ensure that mammalian parents have a strong desire to take care of their offspring. You also see this system active in young children who seem to have a natural affinity to exhibit nurturing behaviors, reflected in a love of animals, certain toys, stuffed animals, or dolls.

Both the CARE system, along with the PANIC system, plays an important role in generating feelings of empathy and sympathy when bad things happen to others, but especially to those we love. It also plays a role in the formation of friendships and the love you feel towards those you are close to.

The LUST/Sexual System in mammals and other types of animals ensures reproduction. In humans, it's imprinted within infant brains during the second trimester. However, the sexual desire generated by this system only becomes fully awakened by the flood of sex hormones that are secreted during adolescence.

The RAGE/Anger system helps an animal protect both itself and the things it needs to survive by attacking threats. This system produces what we normally call anger when it is highly active and irritation when it is only mildly active.

The FEAR/Anxiety system helps all mammals reduce pain and the likelihood of destruction. It promotes freezing in place when danger is far away and flight when it's near. It helps you identify and predict potential threats. It also plays a key role in strengthening memories associated with danger, so it can be avoided in the future. When danger is unavoidable, the RAGE/Anger system activates.

The PANIC/Separation-Distress system is found in all young mammals who depend on maternal care for survival. It is seen in the distress that both human and animal babies show when separated from their caregivers. The cries, prompted by the PANIC system, activate the CARE system in the parent, motivating the parent to find and comfort its baby. You also experience this system with the sadness you feel when separated from loved ones.

While we share the SEEKING, LUST, RAGE, and FEAR emotional systems with reptiles and fish, the CARE, PANIC, and PLAY systems seem to be more uniquely mammalian and give both us and other mammals our more complex social abilities.

Even though the inner part of your brain (the subcortex) has the same structures that generate emotions as other mammals, the outer part where you do your thinking (the cortex) is much larger. In fact, it's the largest part of your brain.

When considering the function of these seven inborn positive and negative emotions, we see that they serve as rewards and punishment that trigger behavior needed to both survive and thrive. Imagine, for example, being stung by hornets flying out of a nest that you accidentally disturbed. Suddenly, you become filled with fear and race away from the nest without the need to think about it. Once a safe distance is reached, and you sense you are out of danger, relief is felt.

The fear associated with this memory will now help you avoid being stung again by causing you to be more vigilant when outdoors. In the same way, behavior that produces positive feelings causes you to want to repeat the behavior. When a parent smiles at a child, it encourages the child to repeat the behavior that caused the parent to smile.

HOW CHILDHOOD SHAPES EMOTIONS

Currently, it is thought that when you were born, the outer portion of your brain where you do your thinking (the cortex) is mostly a blank slate similar to a computer that has yet to be programmed. All the hardware needed for the computer to receive information, do calculations, and display the results is there. However, the instructions needed to coordinate all these activities and make the computer useful are missing.

In the same way, all the structures and neural pathways needed to generate the various emotions you experience are there in the inner part of the brain. However, the outer, thinking part of your brain needs to gain experience and learn how to regulate these systems.

How the thinking part of your brain learns to regulate these emotional systems is influenced by what you experience as a child. The best way to see this is to look at situations where things go terribly wrong. One sad example involves babies that were cared for in orphanages in developing countries that had few resources. These babies would often spend days lying in a crib, cold, and wet. Because there was not enough staff, they were cared for on a schedule. During feeding times, instead of being held, they left the babies in their cribs with the bottles propped up.

As a result, the babies never learned to associate being fed with human contact and warmth. What was even worse was their cries of distress, prompted by the PANIC system, often went unheeded for hours. Their distress became so painful that this system simply shut down. So, while their physical needs were met, these infants did not experience the joy that comes from engaging with another human being or the comfort that comes from having their distress soothed by loving hands. When these babies were adopted, the lack of warm and loving physical contact during infancy made it difficult for them to respond to and bond with their adoptive parents.

A simple experiment involving oxytocin shows how emotional systems in the brain that do not develop properly cause difficulty in bonding. Oxytocin is the hormone associated with both quieting the PANIC system and generating feelings of connection between people through the CARE system.

In this experiment, two groups of mothers with four-year-old children played a simple computer matching game. One group had children and their birth mothers. The other group had children who were neglected as infants and their adoptive mothers. Each mother held her child on her lap as they played the game. They measured oxytocin levels before and after each group played the game. The oxytocin levels in both the birth mothers and the child they raised from birth rose significantly. However, the children who were neglected as infants showed no change in their levels. This nonresponse indicated a lack of development in key emotional systems.

This simple experiment, along with others involving both humans and animals, shows a complex interplay between the emotional systems deep within the brain and the higher thinking portions that develop as an infant grows. So, while children are born with emotional systems designed to help them get the things they need to survive, interact with others, and avoid danger, how these systems develop is shaped by their experiences. A healthy, loving environment that allows a child to play and explore results in the proper development of these systems. Neglectful and abusive environments can cause them to develop in ways that cause problems in later life.

As bleak as this may sound, the good news is that children like this, who later receive proper treatment, can learn how to form stable, healthy bonds with their primary caretakers and others. This shows how adept the brain is at developing new connections. This ability to make new connections is also seen in stroke victims and brain injury victims who have lost the use of certain muscles. With training, the brain is able to reroute and create neural pathways to replace those that were damaged. In the same way, with proper therapy, the higher, executive part of the brain in these children can regain its ability to connect to and manage emotional circuits that had shut down in a more normal way.

The next chapter focuses on how, as a baby grows and develops, the seven basic emotional systems interconnect with the higher functions of the brain to produce what are known as the cognitive emotions: love, guilt, shame, embarrassment, pride, envy, and jealousy. This completes the foundation you need as we turn our attention to the problem of managing emotions that interfere with your life.

SUMMARY OF KEY POINTS

- The term *affect* is used to describe feelings that urge you to act in some way. There are three types: sensory affects, homeostatic affects, and emotional affects

- In the 1990s, Jaak Panksepp coined the term "affective neuroscience," which today is seen as a discipline that studies the brain mechanisms underlying emotions.

- Affective neuroscience has identified seven brain-based emotional action systems in mammals:

Systems that Generate Positive Emotions
SEEKING – Generates an urge to explore and engage with the world with eager curiosity and interest.

LUST – Generates sexual desire

CARE – Produces the desire in parents to care for their offspring

PLAY – Generates the desire for physical play like wrestling, running, and chasing each other in young children. In adults, it generates the various forms of adult play, like playing games and joking.

Systems that Generate Negative Emotions
FEAR – Generates the urge to freeze in place when danger is far away and flight when it's near.

RAGE – Generates the urge to protect yourself by attacking threats. This urge is normally called anger when highly active and irritation when only mildly active.

PANIC – Generates the distress that babies show when separated from their caregivers and the sadness you feel when separated from loved ones.

- The higher thinking part of your brain (the cortex) learns to regulate these emotional systems by what you experience as a child.

- Childhood experiences of neglect and abuse can interfere with the normal development of these systems.

- The brain has a remarkable ability to heal by creating new neurons and rerouting neural pathways.

THINGS TO DO

- Begin to pay attention to times when you are upset or experiencing difficult emotions.

  o Exactly what triggered the emotion?
  o What was going on just before the emotion was triggered?
  o What thoughts and behavior did your emotions generate?

- Answers to these questions will give you material to consider as you work through the following chapters. Some find it helpful to record their answers in a journal so they can more clearly recall them later.

Chapter 2:

The Process that Generates Emotions

Let's not forget that the little emotions are the great captains of our lives, and we obey them without realizing it.

– Vincent van Gogh

In Chapter 1, you learned about the seven core emotional systems deep in your brain. This chapter describes how the higher cognitive emotions emerge from these systems. You'll also learn about the process that triggers emotions and how emotions become associated with memories. First, let's look at some of the activity that goes on in your brain that you are normally unaware of.

YOUR BRAIN ON AUTOPILOT

During the average day, you think about many different things. You recall things from the past, think about events taking place around you, and consider things that may happen in the future. Thoughts that you are aware of like these are called conscious thoughts. While part of your brain is busy with these conscious thoughts, another part of your brain is busy monitoring and coordinating your body and making many different types of decisions about what is going on around you that you're not aware of.

Let's look at what seems to be the simple act of walking. This is actually a very complex activity that requires your brain to do many tasks with every step. Without realizing it, the deeper part of your brain is coordinating muscles and activating them in the correct order, judging distance, identifying and assessing objects that might become obstacles, as well as a host of other things that are necessary to walk. It takes a child many months to learn how to do this. As an adult, however, all this activity takes place with very little conscious thought. You simply look at where you want to go while the conscious part of your brain thinks about things that are often completely unrelated to walking.

Take a moment to consider some of the many things you do that require very little of your attention, such as getting dressed, brushing your teeth, driving, and many of the routine chores you do around the house or at work. Your brain has the amazing ability to learn complex behaviors like these so well that they become automatic. This not only makes life easier, but it also allows you to think about other matters while doing them. This ability of your brain to be aware of your surroundings and make decisions about the events taking place without the need for you to be aware of them plays an important role in many of the emotions you experience.

COGNITIVE MODEL OF EMOTIONS

The word "cognition" refers to thought. Thus, the cognitive model of emotions sees the thoughts you have about events as playing the key role in producing your emotions. Interpreting an event as meeting a need or posing a threat, triggers a corresponding emotion This emotion then urges you to take action. Thus, the sequence of events that produces an emotion is:

- An event takes place
- An interpretation is made as to whether the event meets a need or poses a threat
- If the event meets a need or poses a threat, an emotion is triggered
- The emotion then creates an urge in you to act

This process can be illustrated as:

Event ➡ Interpretation ➡ Emotion ➡ Action

You are fully aware of many of these interpretations–you make a conscious decision as to whether events are meeting a need or posing a threat. For example, a student who wants to do well identifies an upcoming exam as important. The potential threat to the student's grade triggers anxiety that motivates the student to take time to study.

Exam ➡ Threat ➡ Anxiety ➡ Study

Often, however, this interpretation is made by the deeper part of your brain without you being consciously aware of it. This part of your brain is always busy comparing current events with memories of when needs were met or a threat existed. This automatic, unconscious activity is similar to the activity that takes place as you walk and do many other routine activities without the need for you to be aware of them. The way this works is easiest to see with infants whose thinking part of the brain is just beginning to learn how to reason.

Chapter 1 explained how the purpose of the emotional systems you were born with is to drive you to take actions that obtain the things you need to survive and protect you from harm. Babies need food, changing, and a safe and calm environment for healthy development. When a baby is hungry, wet, or alone, the FEAR and PANIC systems create distress that causes the baby to cry. The baby's cry activates the caregiver's CARE system that motivates the caregiver to respond. When the baby is fed, changed, held, or played with, the SEEKING, PLAY, and CARE systems generate positive feelings in the baby as well as bonding with their caregivers. As the baby's memories begin to form, associations are made between events that meet its needs and events that pose a threat.

Because babies are helpless for so long, they need people to take care of them and provide for these basic needs. Thus in addition to the core emotional systems, they are also born with a massive amount of social circuitry for reading other people's faces and behavior. This allows them to quickly learn how to interpret the expressions and body language of caregivers. So, while the interpretation of events in a newborn infant is the result of simple associations, things quickly become more complex as the ability to think and reason develops. We see this with the emergence of cognitive emotions.

COGNITIVE EMOTIONS

Anyone who has observed the first few years of a child's life can't help but be amazed at the changes that occur. The rapid development of the brain allows children to think about and reflect on their emotional experiences as a kind of third-party observer. The addition of spoken language allows for more advanced forms of reasoning and adds further complexity to their emotional experiences. During this time, what are commonly referred to as cognitive emotions gradually emerge. The ones that are most frequently mentioned include love, pride, guilt, shame, embarrassment, envy, and jealousy.

As mentioned above, the word "cognitive" refers to your ability to think and reason. Thus, the cognitive emotions only emerge as rational thought develops, and the thinking part of your brain gains greater ability to influence the deeper, emotional parts. Let's look at the examples of guilt and love to see how this works and why they are called cognitive emotions.

Guilt can be associated with either the CARE or RAGE systems or both, since guilt involves the threat presented to your self-image when you break a personal or societal rule that you believe is important. The realization that you have acted in a way that is different from what you intended can generate regret, a form of sadness. It can also generate anger towards whatever caused you to break the rule. Sometimes you experience both regret and anger. What you experience and how you respond depends both on what you believe to be true and on how you learned to behave while growing up. If, however, you believe the rule is not important or you can justify why it is permissible to break the rule, you will feel no guilt.

With love, we see an association with the CARE emotional system. This system generates bonding in animals and tender feelings in people. The various forms of adult love felt towards a friend, family member, or mate, however, requires the ability to think, reason, and recall events. You need to be able to experience and remember times when this person stood by you during both tragedies and triumphs. There also needs to be times when this person listened with interest as you spoke about the things that are important to you. These and many other experiences form memories with positive feelings associated with them. In addition, these memories become associated with beliefs about love, loyalty, friendship, and similar ideas that you hold. This complex set of associations identifies this person as someone who is important, who meets some or many of your needs, and who generates the tender feelings that the CARE system produces.

Putting all of this together, we see that each of the higher cognitive emotions—love, guilt, shame, embarrassment, pride, envy, and jealousy—require a belief system and the ability to evaluate one's own behavior, others, and one's environment. Because these emotions are shaped by experience and because the rearing of children varies greatly from family to family and culture to culture, it's easy to see why cognitive emotions can be expressed and experienced so differently. This is also why the way people experience these emotions can change as they both practice new behaviors and as their beliefs about others, the world, and themselves change.

This is good news! If you have emotions that are interfering with your life, it's possible to change when and how you experience them. We'll begin to explore some of the ways in which this can be done in the next chapter. For now, let's continue to build our foundation for change and look at an important way in which unconscious associations can generate emotions.

CONDITIONED EMOTIONAL RESPONSES

In the early twentieth century, a Russian scientist named Ivan Petrovich Pavlov coined the term "classical conditioning." Classical conditioning describes a way in which simple automatic responses can be triggered by things that normally have no connection to them. In his experiment, he sounded a bell just before giving hungry dogs food that caused them to salivate. With repetition, the neutral stimulus[4] (the bell) became associated with the food. The salivating of dogs that is normally triggered by the sight or smell of food was now being triggered by something that had no connection to food. This can be summarized as follows:

Inherited automatic response: Food ⟶ Salivate

During conditioning: Bell + Food ⟶ Salivate

Conditioned response: Bell ⟶ Salivate

In the same way, emotional responses can become associated with people, objects, or events that trigger them with no conscious thought. An emotion produced by this type of conditioning is called a conditioned emotional response. A simple example would be a child who enjoys visiting grandparents. Now, imagine that part of the fun at the grandparents' house is baking and eating chocolate chip cookies. If this experience is repeated many times, the positive feelings experienced with the grandparents become associated with baking and eating chocolate chip cookies. As an adult, it would

---

[4] A neutral stimulus in classical conditioning is something that has no relation to the response we want to associate with it. In the example here, the bell has no relationship to salivation that is normally triggered by the sight, smell, or taste of food.

not be surprising to find that this person's favorite type of cookie is chocolate chip. We might even discover that this person buys them when feeling sad in order to feel better.

Classical conditioning and conditioned emotional responses play a major, though usually unrecognized, role in your daily life. Many of your preferences and dislikes result from the conditioning you experienced when you were young. Think of the types of food you like to eat. You probably enjoy food you are familiar with and often do not like food that differs from what you know. Because you have been conditioned to enjoy the sights, odors, and tastes of food you are familiar with, they trigger a positive response when you are hungry.

However, the sights, odors, and tastes of unfamiliar foods or spices may produce the opposite reaction. Just the sight of people eating some foods, such as snakes, grubs, or insects, may even sicken you while others find their mouths watering at the sight of such delicacies. The same can be said of the music you enjoy, as well as many aspects of how you approach work, what you find entertaining, and what attracts you to others.

EMOTIONAL "TAGS"

Children have a wide variety of experiences where they feel pleasure, pain, threat, and loss. The emotions they experience at these times become part of the memories that form about these events and begin the process of creating conditioned emotional responses.

Memories of events that are painful or pleasurable are created with the emotion that was experienced associated with them. I will call the emotions that are connected to specific memories "emotional tags." Positive emotional tags became connected to memories of events like the pleasure you experienced when discovering a new ability or when you saw joy on the face of caregivers as you did something that pleased them. Negative emotional tags became attached to memories of unpleasant events, such as the pain of being bitten by a dog when you pulled its tail or seeing a look of disappointment when you did something that displeased your caregivers.

Having memories associated with emotions helps your mind sort them according to their importance. Memories that are important have a stronger emotional tag than those that are less important. Some information has no emotion associated with it.

To understand how the brain uses emotional tags to sort memories of events and information, consider Tarah, who is learning to drive. She can read about driving and watch videos; however, it's not until she is behind the wheel of a car that her brain can sort this information into important and less important categories. Emotional tags are created both by the fear that strikes when the car goes the wrong way or does something unexpected and by the pleasure experienced when the car responds as she wishes. These tags then help her take the proper actions needed when driving in the future. This explains why book knowledge needs to be combined with experience for it to be useful. Experience allows your mind to identify important information and use it as a guide for future interpretations and actions.

At this point in your life, you have countless associations, beliefs, and information with varying emotional tags that are shaping how you react to events. An unconscious part of your mind is always scanning your environment and the events taking place around you.

Whenever something is noticed that has, in the past, been given an emotional tag, either positive or negative, it triggers the associated emotion. The stronger the tag, the stronger the emotion.

The emotion that was triggered then draws your attention to whatever is triggering it. For example, if you are reading a book and suddenly hear a loud crash, all thoughts about what you are reading are quickly replaced with the desire to know what caused the crash. In the past, this type of sound was associated with danger. So, the emotional tag connected to unexplained loud sounds quickly focuses your awareness on it and urges you to identify whether it's safe or dangerous.

SIMPLIFYING TERMINOLOGY

Because the SEEKING, CARE, PLAY, and LUST systems play less of a role in the most common emotional problems, from this point on I'll focus on the FEAR, RAGE, and PANIC systems. While the word fear makes the FEAR emotional system easy to understand, the labels for the RAGE and PANIC systems are not as clear. Since the RAGE emotional system generates the various forms of anger we experience, I'll use the word anger when discussing emotions associated with the RAGE system.

The PANIC emotional system was given its name because it generates the extreme distress that both baby animals and young children experience when separated from their caregivers. As children grow and this system becomes interconnected with the outer thinking parts of the developing brain, it underlies the various forms of sadness we experience with loss. So, I'll refer to the emotions generated by the PANIC emotional system as sadness.

Fear – FEAR emotional system
Anger – RAGE emotional system
Sadness – PANIC emotional system

As you see the words fear, anger and sadness in future chapters, keep in mind that I'm using each word to represent a broad range of emotions. In the case of fear, we use many different words to describe the types of fear we experience, but on closer examination, we are just describing different levels of the same emotion. "Apprehension" is used to describe a very low level of fear, while "terror" describes the extreme level of fear we might feel in a life-threatening situation.

In the same way, "irritation" is used to describe what you might feel when faced with a minor inconvenience, while "rage" describes the anger that a person might experience when protecting a loved one in a life-threatening situation. With sadness, "disappointment" is used to describe the sadness you experience with a minor loss, while "depression" describes the deep distress you might experience with the death of a loved one. The range of these emotions can be illustrated as:

Apprehension ————— Fear ——————Terror
Irritation ———————Anger ——————— Rage
Disappointment ——— Sadness ——— Depression

Now, let's look at the interpretations that trigger each of these three emotions: the presence of a threat or loss. Fear and anger are the two basic responses we have to a perceived[5] threat. Fear is generated when the threat is perceived as unmanageable, such as when a large bear is approaching. Anger is generated when the threat is

---

[5] Perceived: your belief about something that may or may not be based on reality.

Threat
Fear (Unmanageable Threat)
Anger (Manageable Threat)

Loss ⟶ Sadness

perceived as manageable, such as when a small dog is barking at you. Sadness is generated when you experience a loss.

Notice that I used the word "perceived" in the above because we sometimes see threat or loss in a situation when there is no real threat or loss. For example, most would be comfortable being introduced to a new group of people. However, a shy or insecure person might see being introduced to new people as a threat and experience anxiety, maybe even fear.

Since there is little threat or loss associated with many of your daily activities, much of your conscious thought, such as thinking about what clothes you are going to wear, generates little, if any, emotion. However, the deeper part of your mind is always on the alert for indications that a need will be satisfied or that a threat or loss exists. Whenever this part of your mind—the autopilot discussed at the beginning of the chapter—becomes aware of the satisfaction of a need, a threat, or loss, the corresponding emotion is generated. This expanded cognitive model can be diagrammed as follows:

Event ⟶ Interpretation ⟶ A need has been or may be satisfied ⟶ Various positive emotions such as joy, excitement, or feeling close to someone

A threat exists or may soon exist ⟶ Anger (manageable threat) or fear (unmanageable threat)

A loss has occured ⟶ Sadness, grief, or depression

While you see these responses most clearly in young children, this quickly becomes more complicated. As one's ability to reason develops, the cognitive emotions emerge along with a belief system about oneself, others, and the world. This might cause a person who has experienced the loss of something important to experience anger instead of sadness. Those who believe that life should be fair might focus on resenting whatever caused the loss. The reason for the loss is now being attacked instead of experiencing the loss and, generates anger.

Others might have learned to always be strong and in control. This makes the helplessness that is felt with loss intolerable. So, finding something to focus on that generates anger helps them have a physical sensation of strength as adrenaline triggered by anger surges through their body. This allows them to avoid feeling the helplessness that often accompanies the sadness of loss. Much more will be said about the way we sometimes hide from emotions that have become unacceptable and the price we pay for doing this in a later chapter.

In the next chapter, you will learn how the interpretations made by this deeper part of your mind combine with the thoughts that you are aware of in the thinking part of your brain. The first tools for quieting emotions that might interfere with your life are also presented.

SUMMARY OF KEY POINTS

- The cognitive model of emotions sees emotions as being generated in the following manner: an event takes place; an interpretation is made as to whether the event poses a threat, loss, or meets a need; an emotion is triggered that creates an urge in you to take action that corresponds to the interpretation.

- The cognitive emotions include love, guilt, shame, embarrassment, pride, envy, and jealousy. They emerged as your ability to think and reason developed during childhood.

- The expression of cognitive emotions can vary widely from family to family and culture to culture because beliefs and experiences can be very different.

- Much of your interpretation of events is done unconsciously.

- Conditioned emotional responses are the automatic triggering of an emotion by the deeper part of your brain in response to a person, thing, or situation.

- Memories concerning needs have emotional tags associated with them. The more important the memory, the stronger the emotion associated with it. This helps your brain sort important information from less important information.

- From this point on, the words fear, anger, and sadness will be used when talking about the FEAR, RAGE, and PANIC emotional systems. Keep in mind that each represents a broad range of emotions.

- Negative emotions are triggered by a perceived threat or loss. A threat that is perceived as unmanageable triggers fear. A threat that is perceived as manageable triggers anger. Loss triggers sadness.

THINGS TO DO

- Continue to pay attention to times when you are upset or experiencing difficult emotions. Take special notice of the automatic nature of many of your negative emotions. As with the activity you began in Chapter 1, continue to note:

o Exactly what triggered the emotion?

o What was going on just before the emotion was triggered?

o What thoughts and behavior did your emotions generate?

o When possible, identify the specific threat or loss that generated a negative emotion.

o Do any of the threats or losses you identified have roots in your childhood experiences?

Answers to these questions will give you material to consider as you work through the following chapters. Some find it helpful to record their answers in a journal so they can more clearly recall them later.

• Take some time to think about the events during your childhood that helped to shape your beliefs about people, relationships, and the world. If you have emotional responses that are causing difficulties, look for connections with your childhood experiences. Again, many find it helpful to record their thoughts in a journal so they can more clearly recall them later when we look at ways to change emotional responses that are interfering with your life.

Chapter 3:

Emotional Triggers

A trigger is the connection between the conscious mind and a buried painful memory.

– William (Bill) Tollefson

C hapter 2 explained how many of the positive and negative emotions you experience each day are simple conditioned emotional responses like the excitement of anticipating a favorite food or the disgust of seeing food that differs greatly from what you know. This chapter looks at responses that are the result of trauma. These are intense negative emotions that are either not logically connected to the events taking place around you or are much more intense than would be expected. Along with this, an approach for quieting these disruptive responses is explored.

EMOTIONAL TRIGGERS

The previous chapter described how the emotional tags associated with danger shifts your attention from whatever you are doing to the potential threat. They also prepare your body to take action through the fight-or-flight response. To do this, conditioned emotional responses associated with danger can be very strong.

Having a quick and strong response to potential threats has been essential for human survival, especially when we lived in more primitive conditions. If a certain sight, sound, smell, or touch meant danger, it needed an immediate response. This response still helps people respond quickly to potential harm, whether they are in a war zone or simply driving to work.

Unfortunately, a conditioned emotional response that is generated in response to danger can live on long after the danger has passed. When this happens, the emotional response associated with the past threat will now be triggered by daily events that pose no threat.

Sandy and James were both on a plane that was struck by lightning while in the air. There was a deafening bang as the plane shook violently. People were screaming and crying, and Sandy and James were both shaken. Just after the strike, the pilot announced they had lost one engine and were going to make an emergency landing. The plane was quickly rerouted and landed with no further incident. However, as they left by a set of exit stairs that had been rolled up, they could see two large areas on the outside of the plane that were black from the lightning strike.

Sandy and James both flew frequently because of their work, and both experienced anxiety as they prepared for their next trip. The experience with the lightning strike had connected a strong emotional tag of fear to flying. Just the sight or thought of an airplane became an emotional trigger–a conditioned emotional response of anxiety–that both Sandy and James experienced as they prepared for and boarded their next flight.

Sandy found her anxiety faded after several fights, and she no longer experienced anxiety before, during, or after a flight. James, however, found that the anxiety he experienced increased so much with his next three flights that he quit flying altogether.

Why did Sandy have such a different experience from James following the lightning strike? The answer can be found in something called desensitization.

DESENSITIZATION

Desensitization can be understood by revisiting the example of classical conditioning in Chapter 2 where a bell triggers salivation in dogs.

Inherited automatic response:		Food ⟶	Salivate
During conditioning:	Bell +	Food ⟶	Salivate
Conditioned response:		Bell ⟶	Salivate

After establishing a strong response to the bell, if you continue to ring it but no longer give the dogs food afterwards, they will eventually stop salivating at the sound of the bell. The process where a conditioned response stops because it is no longer reinforced is called desensitization. In the same way, a conditioned emotional response will fade if it is not reinforced.

When Sandy was preparing for her next few flights after the lightning strike, she calmed herself by remembering that no harm came to her, and that flying is extremely safe. She also reminded herself that this was a once-in-a-lifetime event and that flying would become more comfortable each time she flew. As a result, after a few flights, she no longer experienced anxiety. Sandy had desensitized herself to flying by calming herself each time it triggered the conditioned response.

In contrast, however, James dwelt on frightening thoughts about being on a plane that crashed and being burned to death. He also exaggerated the danger of the lightning strike and told himself that he had only narrowly escaped death. Dwelling on negative images and repeating frightening self-talk like this reinforced the conditioned emotional response created by the lightning strike.

This is a key point as it explains how emotional triggers can be quieted or kept alive. Calming and reassuring yourself each time they occur allows them to quiet down. Reacting with alarm and fearful thoughts each time they occur strengthens them. While this principle is easy to understand, its application can be difficult.

OUR BRAIN IS NOT A COMPUTER

One difficulty in helping people quiet a conditioned emotional response through the process of desensitization, is that the brain is often compared to a computer. People use terms like "reprogramming" and "deleting files" to describe the process of changing negative thinking patterns and self-defeating behavior. However, the brain is not a computer; it's an organic system made of living cells and connections that change through growth and development. It's not a set of wires, transistors, and memory chips where you can overwrite a program or delete a file with a single action.

To understand this better, let's look at how memories are normally formed. Imagine yourself walking through a dense rainforest that has thick underbrush for the first time. As you proceed, a path is created as grass is stepped on and you cut away branches from the underbrush that are in the way. If you use the path frequently, it becomes clearer and easier to follow. If you quit using it, even a well-worn path will disappear. However, just as the return of the path to the forest takes time, the same is true of quieting a strong, conditioned emotional response.

The cells that make up your brain circuits work in a similar manner to the creation of the path in the forest. While we don't know all the details, connections between nerves involved with memories that are used frequently grow stronger and easier to access. They're like a muscle that gets stronger with use. We can see this when learning a complex new skill that involves memory, such as learning a language. It takes time and repetition before both the grammar and vocabulary associated with the new language becomes so automatic that your conscious mind no longer needs to pay much attention when speaking it. With time, however, even the strong connections between nerves associated with memories and skills fade if not used.

You can see this in people who were born in a non-English-speaking country who then lived in an English-speaking country for many years and only spoke English. Even if they only began using English as a teenager, twenty or thirty years later they often find it difficult to speak the native language they learned as a child, if they did not use it as an adult.

Something that affects the speed of both the creation and the fading of a memory is the level of emotion attached to it. The more intense the emotion, the stronger and more enduring the memory. It's like having several people help you create the path in your imaginary forest. This is why it's easy to remember things you are interested in and excited about, while things of little interest are quickly forgotten.

Unfortunately, this also means that the pathway created by a terrifying event, like the lightning strike, is like having a bulldozer carve a path through your imaginary forest. The path is wide and easy to find. However, just like any of the other paths, it will fade if it is not used. In the same way, desensitization takes time, but it does work! Understanding this can keep you from getting discouraged in a world of quick fixes and instant results. Desensitization takes time, but it works!

WHAT'S HAPPENING, WHAT'S REAL

In the earlier example of Sandy and James, we saw Sandy did not reinforce the conditioned emotional response associated with flying by telling herself things that calmed her. At the same time, James reinforced it with his fearful reaction and frightening thoughts. A simple but effective way to calm yourself and stop reinforcing distressing emotional triggers is:

- Tell yourself what's happening
- Tell yourself what's real
- Shift your thoughts to something positive.

Here is an example of the type of self-talk Sandy used when she felt anxious about flying:

What's Happening

The anxiety I'm experiencing is because of the lightning strike I experienced and is a simple conditioned emotional response. It's a normal unconscious reaction to a frightening event and will fade over time.

What's Real

While the lightning strike was very frightening, it was a once-in-a-lifetime experience, and no harm came to me. While I thought I was in danger at the time, planes that get struck by lightning can land safely, just like mine did. It's also true that millions of people fly every day with no problems. In fact, I'm safer on a plane than I am driving home.

Positive Shift

Now, let's focus on getting my things together and preparing for tomorrow's meeting.

Shifting your thoughts to something positive is most effective if it involves physical activity such as doing a household or work-related chore, talking with someone you like, or engaging in some form of play with a friend, child, or pet.

During and after going through desensitization, keep in mind that old patterns can reawaken when the right set of circumstances are encountered. Returning to Pavlov's work with dogs, he tried yet another experiment with dogs that had been conditioned to salivate to the sound of a bell. He then rang the bell periodically with no food, so the bell no longer triggered salivation. They had been desensitized to the bell.

After waiting for some time, he then again rang the bell. This sudden reintroduction of the trigger caused the dogs to salivate again. However, with repeated rings, they quickly stopped responding and again became desensitized. In the same way, a conditioned emotional response that has quieted can sometimes reawaken unexpectedly when an old trigger is encountered.

A year after her experience on the plane, there was a thunderstorm the night before a flight that Sandy was going to take. She experienced anxiety like what she had felt after the lightning strike both that night and when she approached the airport the next day. If she had reacted with alarm, it would have caused the old, conditioned response to increase. Instead, she realized what was happening and told herself:

What's Happening

I'm surprised by my anxiety. However, it's probably just due to all the thunder and lightning last night that reminded me of that flight last year.

What's Real

This is not a big deal. I quickly became comfortable flying last year and these feelings will disappear if I don't give them any attention.

Positive Shift

Let's just continue packing and thinking about my plans for tomorrow.

As Sandy got busy, she relaxed. In the same way, if an old pattern reemerges, use the same desensitization process you used when you originally quieted it. Also, keep in mind that old patterns most often reemerge when you are sick, hungry, tired, under unusual stress, or dealing with something related to the original incident that generated it.

THE ROLE OF INSIGHT

One roadblock that people sometimes hit when quieting triggers is the belief that once you understand why you are being triggered, the conditioned emotional response should quiet down on its own. In other words, you only need insight to resolve an emotional issue. I've seen this cause much confusion and distress in clients who say things such as, "I understand why I'm reacting this way. So why does it keep happening?"

The answer is that the automatic part of the brain you learned about in Chapter 2 that manages routine tasks like walking also generates conditioned emotional responses like the ones described in this chapter. When this part of the brain detects anything associated with danger, it fires the fight-or-flight response without involving the conscious part of your brain. Often, this response is experienced as anxiety.

In Sandy's case, this deeper part of the brain had connected an emotional tag of danger to the sights and sounds of lightning and flying. This tag was activating her anxiety on flights right after the lightning strike. The only way to quiet this response was for this deeper part of the brain to learn to reassociate flying with safety. This is where the conscious, thinking part of the brain came in. By calming and reassuring herself each time the automatic, unconscious part of the brain reacted, the deeper part of her brain learned to once again associate flying with safety instead of danger.

DEEPLY EMBEDDED EMOTIONAL TRIGGERS

The emotional trigger that developed in Sandy and James was due to a single experience. Often, however, emotional triggers are because of difficult childhood or adult circumstances such as an abusive relationship or being in an environment where there was continuous violence, such as combat.

Each year after leaving home, Ellie became anxious as Thanksgiving approached. While her anxiety would decrease some during the next week, it would then increase even more as Christmas drew near. Let's look at what caused her "holiday anxiety."

Ellie grew up in a family where both parents were alcoholics. As a result, there was frequent fighting and tension in the house. Each year saw lots of drinking and arguing during Thanksgiving. Things would then quiet for a while, but as Christmas approached, drinking and fights about money and other holiday-related issues would increase along with the verbal abuse that Ellie experienced. As this occurred, the holiday decorations, music, and activities all became associated with the increased tension and danger in the house. This caused them to become triggers warning of increased danger during this time of the year. As an adult, these deeply embedded associations caused the trappings of the holiday season to continue to signal the approach of danger even though it no longer existed.

After Ellie understood what was causing her holiday anxiety, she began to calm herself with the "what's happening, what's real" approach. She found it helpful to write three statements on cards she could read once a day for several days until she could paraphrase each one without much thought. Then, she would repeat them to herself whenever she noticed her anxiety was increasing.

I call cards like these "Rational Thought Cards" because they provide a brief summary of your understanding of 1) why you are being triggered, 2) specific things you can tell yourself that will calm the distressing emotions being triggered by the past, and 3) a reminder to shift your thoughts to something positive. Here is what Ellie wrote on her "Rational Thought Card."

HOLIDAY ANXIETY

What's Happening

I'm experiencing a conditioned emotional response that was caused by the frightening things that occurred in my home during the holidays. Mom and Dad became more abusive, and I was constantly on the alert so I would stay out of their way and under their radar.

What's Real

I'm now an adult and safe in my own home. I am able to set healthy boundaries and no longer need to be afraid of what my parents might do. I control what happens here and can make the holidays into whatever I want.

Positive Shift

Be confident and assertive with my holiday plans. I can choose to do activities that bring joy. Now, get busy with something I like. I can do it.

In addition to using this technique, Ellie was also working on negative beliefs and behaviors that developed during her childhood, along with ways to take care of herself more effectively. So, even though Ellie's anxiety returned the next year, it was not as intense and easier to dismiss. As explained earlier, this is normal, as it often takes time to quiet old responses.

In the following years, she enjoyed the holidays with only occasional anxiety. When this happened, she used the "what's happening, what's real" approach to calm herself. She also learned that the recurrence of anxiety was often a message that she needed to slow down and take care of physical or emotional needs or address an important life problem she had been ignoring. This type of work is discussed in later chapters.

IDENTIFYING TRIGGERS

It's common to have several types of people, things, or situations associated with the intense feelings of anxiety, anger, or sadness experienced during trauma. This is especially true for trauma that was experienced over a long period. So, the first step in calming these feelings is to identify the specific things that trigger them. While the many things and events that become emotional triggers are too numerous to list, common examples include:

- encountering people, things, or events that remind you of painful past experiences
- disapproval or criticism
- feeling unwanted or unneeded
- intimacy
- rejection (real or imagined)
- unjust treatment
- challenged beliefs

- helplessness or loss of control
- being excluded or ignored

If you are having trouble, identifying the specific things and events that are acting as triggers, pay attention to early physical symptoms that indicate you are being triggered, such as:

- pounding heart
- upset stomach
- shakiness or dizziness
- sweaty palms

When you notice symptoms like these, identify what was going on when you experienced them. Then, try following these feelings back to their origins by recalling situations in your past that were similar to the one that triggered the current feelings. You can also recall situations in the past that made you feel what you're currently feeling and look for connections between the past and the present.

If you're in a situation where you need to pay attention to what's going on around you, such as driving or being at work, take time later to reflect on what was happening as you were feeling the emotions that were being triggered. The goal is to identify things in the current situation that are like things in your past that triggered similar emotions.

Sometimes, the connection isn't clear, and you may have to do some digging. The best way to do this when strong emotions come up is to resist any urge to fight or ignore them. Instead, try to observe your reaction as if you were outside of yourself. Maintain, as best as you are able, an attitude of curiosity. As you do this over time, ask yourself if any patterns stand out. For example, do discussions with a certain person or a certain topic cause sadness, anger, or anxiety? Do certain types of scenes in movies or television programs trigger intense emotion? The more specific you are, the more successful you will be.

If you have emotional triggers that you want to quiet, keep in mind that while the approach described in this chapter can be effective, it often needs to be combined with the types of work described in the following chapters.

The next chapter explores how these unconscious conditioned responses are affected by your inherited temperament and become intertwined with your conscious thoughts and beliefs.

SUMMARY OF KEY POINTS

- Triggers can be almost anything, such as a word, a person, a certain type of situation or touch, even an odor. They trigger a conditioned emotional response in the form of an intense negative emotion that's either not logically connected to the events taking place around you or much more intense than would normally be appropriate.

- These types of triggers are the result of trauma. They are part of your brain's mechanism to warn you of potential danger.

- Desensitization is the process of quieting a conditioned emotional response by calming yourself whenever it is triggered.

- The brain is not a computer. You do not "reprogram" or "delete files" in a simple single action.

- The brain is made up of living cells and connections that change through growth and development. This takes time.

- The "what's happening, what's real" approach is:

  o Tell yourself what's happening

  o Tell yourself what's real

  o Shift your thoughts to something positive.

- While this approach can be very effective in quieting emotional triggers, it often needs to be combined with other types of work to be most effective.

THINGS TO DO

- If you experience conditioned emotional responses that intrude into your life, use the ideas presented in this chapter to identify specific triggers and the connections they have with the past.

- As you find connections, use the "what's happening, what's real" approach to calm yourself. If you have difficulty, try writing out your response and read it once a day for a few days.

Chapter 4:

Core Response Patterns

Just as the twig is bent the tree's inclined.

– Early 18th Century
English Proverb

T his chapter looks at how the genes inherited from parents interact with events that take place during childhood. It then describes how core response patterns shape the emotions you experience, as well as your ability to achieve the goals you have in life.

THE DUNEDIN STUDY

A study by the University of Otago Dunedin School of Medicine has provided us with some of the best information available on the interaction between a person's genes and the environment. The study has followed the lives of 1,037 babies born between April 1, 1972, and March 31, 1973 at Queen Mary Maternity Hospital, Dunedin, New Zealand, since their birth. Every year, each person's medical history, temperament, genes, private life, success, and failures are carefully looked at and recorded.

Even now, six decades after the study started, 97% of the original group is still part of the study. The study has produced over 1,300 publications and reports, and its findings have been found valid in studies conducted in a wide variety of countries and populations.

One area that is of particular interest to us is the five basic personality types that were identified in the babies they were studying. These types were first clearly identified at the age of three years old and were seen to persist into adulthood. They were labeled: confident, well-adjusted, reserved, inhibited, and undercontrolled.

The confident type makes up about 28% of the population. As babies, this group was exceptionally friendly, somewhat impulsive, eager to explore, and displayed little or no concern about separating from their caregiver. As adults, they enjoy dangerous and exciting experiences and activities and are not afraid to take on challenges.

The well-adjusted group was the most common type and made up about 40% of the children. As children, they were capable of self-control when it was demanded of them, adequately self-confident, and open to new experiences. As adults, they are flexible, resourceful, and fit in well socially.

Children in the confident and well-adjusted groups usually grew up to be productive members of society. Their positive traits allowed them to do well in life. They were more likely to be happily married, have friends, and have good health.

They labeled the third group, reserved. This group made up about 15% of the children. As babies they were timid but not to the point of being paralyzed by it. As adults they tend to be quiet with a natural tendency to sit back and watch rather than interact. This is especially true in new situations. In a healthy loving family, they were able to overcome this natural tendency and do well in life.

The final two groups are the inhibited and undercontrolled groups. As adults these two groups experienced the most trouble and anguish for themselves and the rest of society.

The inhibited group only made up about 7% of the population. As babies they were fearful, easily upset, and reluctant to participate socially with others. As adults they are fearful, anxious, don't like change, tend to be high-strung, and are more prone to depression.

The undercontrolled group made up about 10% of the population. As children, they were impulsive, restless, negative, and distractible. As adults, they don't like change and tend to be antisocial and prone to unemployment. They struggle with self-control, fighting, and drug use. Thus, it was not surprising to find a higher rate of heart disease, diabetes, lung problems, and sexually transmitted diseases in the adults of this group.

The good news from this study is that the future of these groups was not dependent on their personality alone. In healthy families, even the children in the last two groups could learn skills that increased their future health, wealth, and happiness. Likewise, children in all the groups raised in dysfunctional families had problems later in life. So, regardless of your background and the difficult emotions that you may now struggle with, it's possible to learn new behaviors and ways of thinking that enable you to be successful and enjoy life.

THE INFLUENCE OF FAMILY ON GENES

While much is still to be done, many genes have been identified as playing a role in a wide variety of problems. They include medical problems associated with a single gene, such as cystic fibrosis and sickle cell anemia, to problems where multiple genes interact with lifestyle, such as cancer and heart disease. The same has been shown to be true of several emotional problems.

One striking example was the role that a gene known as MAOA plays in violent behavior. This gene helps regulate hormones that affect mood, behavior, and a person's response to stress. It has two forms: a short form associated with lower levels of these hormones and a long form associated with higher levels of these hormones. While the short form is common in adults who are violent criminals, this is not the entire story.

The Dunedin studies found that the gene by itself did not predict violent behavior at all. Likewise, it found that maltreatment during childhood was also not a very good predictor. It was the combination that predicted violent antisocial behavior in adults. In fact, 85% of the individuals with the short version of the gene who were severely mistreated exhibited antisocial behavior by the time they were adults.

This interaction was underscored by a discovery made by Dr. James Fallon, an American neuroscientist who was looking at PET scans of violent prisoners. Out of curiosity, he looked at his own along with those of his family and found that they were the same as the violent criminals he was studying. He also found he had the short form of the MAOA gene. When he researched his family history, he found that it included seven alleged murderers, including Lizzie Borden, infamously accused of killing her father and stepmother in 1892.

Dr. Fallon admits, "I'm obnoxiously competitive. I won't let my grandchildren win games. I'm kind of an a – hole."[6] He also says that he sometimes does things just to annoy people. At the same time, he is happily married with children and leads a normal life. He believes that, while he's aggressive, his aggression is sublimated. "I'd rather beat someone in an argument than beat them up." He attributes this to the fact that, "I was loved, and that protected me." Because a series of miscarriages preceded his birth, he believes his parents gave him an especially heavy amount of attention, and he thinks that played a key role in his turning out O.K.

It's now known that about 30% of the population has the weak form of the MAOA gene. Yet most, like Dr. Fallon, become productive members of society, leading normal lives. This means that while you may have a genetic push in one direction or another, the influence of childhood plays a major role in shaping how that push is expressed. In addition, as an adult, you can make choices and learn to modify how you think and behave to soften the effects of both your genes and childhood background.

Dr. Fallon states, "Since finding all this out and looking into it, I've made an effort to try to change my behavior. I've more consciously been doing things that are considered 'the right thing to do,' and thinking more about other people's feelings. At the same time, I'm not doing this because I'm suddenly nice; I'm doing it because of pride– because I want to show to everyone and myself that I can pull it off."

---

[6] Stromberg, Joseph, *Smithsonian magazine*, Nov. 22, 2013.

CORE RESPONSE PATTERNS

During childhood, the various associations that developed both influenced and were influenced by the beliefs you came to hold about yourself, others, and the world around you. This interaction resulted in what I will call core response patterns. These are a collection of both unconscious conditioned emotional responses and conscious beliefs that cause you to react to others or the world in a specific way. A simple example of this is called one's locus of control[7].

The term, "locus of control", refers to how much control individuals believe they have over the events that influence their lives. This belief is then used to determine why they succeeded or failed at something. The two categories that are usually described are an internal or external locus of control. People who base their success on their own work and believe they control their life have an internal locus of control. In contrast, people who attribute their success or failure to outside influences have an external locus of control.

When people with an internal locus of control gain a promotion or succeed at something, they usually see their success as a direct result of their hard work. If they fail at something, they find a way to blame themselves for the perceived failure. For example, they might believe that they didn't work hard enough.

People with an external locus of control tend to attribute a promotion or success to external or environmental factors, such as luck, fate, timing, other people, or some type of divine intervention.

---

[7] The word "locus" refers to the place where something is situated or occurs. The term "locus of control" was created by Julian B. Rotter in 1954 and quickly became a central concept in the field of personality psychology.

When they don't get a promotion or fail at something, it's easy, even natural, to blame outside sources beyond their control. For example, they might think that being passed over for a promotion was because the manager has favorite employees, and they are not one of them.

When looking at a core response pattern like locus of control, keep in mind that these are two opposite ends of a continuum. A person's thinking and emotions may reflect an external locus of control in some areas and an internal locus of control in others. For example, Ellie often felt at the mercy of external forces in many areas of her life.

However, one area where she felt she had control was in the selection of a partner. Because her parents abused alcohol, she did not drink at all. She also knew that she wanted a partner who felt the same way as she did. This was something that attracted her to her husband when they met.

SELF-EFFICACY

Another well-known core response pattern is called self-efficacy. Albert Bandura coined this term in 1977, and it became a central concept in his social cognitive theory. Self-efficacy is the belief that individuals have concerning their ability to take actions that allow them to succeed in a particular situation. Your level of self-efficacy plays a major role in how you view yourself and can help or block your ability to achieve important life goals.

People with a high level of self-efficacy see themselves as having the ability to take action that achieves success. As a result, they develop a deeper interest in the activities in which they participate and form a stronger sense of commitment to their interests and activities. They also recover more quickly from setbacks and disappointments. When they look at challenging problems, they simply see them as tasks to be mastered.

People with a weak sense of self-efficacy tend to avoid challenging tasks because they believe that difficult tasks and situations are beyond their ability. They tend to focus on personal failings and negative outcomes and quickly lose confidence in personal abilities.

Self-efficacy has been an important concept in education, as students with a high level are confident in their ability to learn and do well on tests. Students with a weak sense of self-efficacy often fail to put in the effort needed to learn because they see it as something that is beyond them. This sets up a pattern of failure that has major consequences both for educators and for society.

One's sense of self-efficacy and one's locus of control generate different types of emotions because they influence how you interpret events and influence the conditioned emotional responses that developed during childhood. People with an external locus of control and weak sense of self-efficacy tend to experience emotions such as depression over the perceived hopelessness of the situation, anger at themselves for being so useless, anger at the apparent source of their difficulties, or anxiety over what may happen. At the same time, individuals with an internal locus of control and high level of self-efficacy usually face challenges with more positive emotions and confidence in their ability to overcome the challenge.

While environmental factors play an important role in the development of core response patterns like these, genetics also play a role. It is much easier for a child who is reserved or inhibited to develop these patterns than one who is confident.

TAKING A CLOSER LOOK AT THE FORCES THAT CREATE CORE RESPONSE PATTERNS

To understand more fully how the various things discussed in the previous chapters combine to produce the two core response patterns discussed in this chapter–locus of control and self-efficacy–we'll take an in depth look at Ellie, who you first met in Chapter 3. This will begin with a brief description of the people who played an important role during her childhood along with a set of early recollections.

A genogram is placed at the beginning of Ellie's profile to help you visualize the relationships between the important people in Ellie's life when she was a child. The squares in each genogram represent males, and the circles represent females. A horizontal line represents a marriage. The vertical line drawn to Ellie is a little longer than those drawn to her brothers to make Ellie stand out from her siblings. Children are listed from the oldest to the youngest.

The genogram is followed by a brief description of each adult who played an important role in Ellie's childhood and a set of early recollections from grade school, middle school, high school, and early adulthood. Early recollections are a brief general description of what life was like at that time.

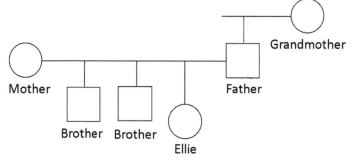

Mother

Mother worked as a waitress in various local chain restaurants. She was quiet and had little social life. After work, she would have two or three glasses of wine, clean up, then watch television. She usually was in bed by 8 p.m. She rarely had anything positive to say and was quick to point out mistakes.

Father

Father worked as a plumber for the city. When he came home, he would drink several beers each night. He liked sports and, on the weekends, would often spend his time at a local bar watching whatever games were playing with a small group of friends. When angry, he was loud and could be a little scary. We didn't have much of a relationship. Father often talked about how unfair things were, and that a person can't get ahead even if they try.

Grandmother (Father's Mom)

Grandma would babysit us when we were young. She was very old-fashioned and strict, but she had a warm heart. She was someone I could talk to about anything. I think I had a special place in her heart because I was the only girl.

Early Recollections

Childhood through Grade School

On weekends, we would often go to the park or beach. At first my parents didn't drink much, so we could enjoy being out of our apartment. Gradually, our outings were accompanied by more drinking. By the end of the outing, there would be lots of bickering. At home, things would start out quiet. Around dinner time there would be verbal fights that would then quiet down as both parents went their separate ways. Father would watch television in the front room while mother had her own television in the bedroom.

During grade School I would sometimes spend the weekend with grandmother. She lived about an hour away from my parents. Since my brothers preferred being with their friends, it was just the two of us. These were wonderful times. While she was very strict, she loved my company. She would fix my hair and we would cook and play cards or watch television.

My brothers teased me a lot. They often told me how stupid I was because I couldn't do some of the things they did. Because I was the youngest, I didn't realize that it was just because I was younger. I really thought I wasn't that bright.

I was not much of a student at school, as my family didn't see learning as very important. My dad used to tell the boys, "Learn a trade like I did, and work with your hands. That way, you'll always have food on the table." At school, I was only getting C's and D's. This also caused me to think that I wasn't very smart.

Middle School

The fighting increased at home between my parents. My brothers continued to tease me about being slow. However, they were gone a lot, so there was less of this. Whenever I could, I would go to my grandmother's house to escape from the chaos at home. However, these times became fewer as she felt ill more and more often.

The kids at school made fun of anyone who did well, so I just did enough to get by and fit in with the crowd. I especially remember struggling with math.

High School

Grandmother died just before I entered high school. I missed her a lot, as the times I was with her were a peaceful oasis away from the turmoil at home. I began hanging out at my friends' houses to escape from home. This was especially true on the weekend, when there were always lots of loud fights between my parents. However, things were quieter during the week, as they both just drank and sank into their own little worlds. On the bright side, the fighting was never physical. They just yelled a lot at each other.

Early Adult

After graduating from high school, I began working as a waitress like my mother. When I was twenty, I married a cook at one of the restaurants where I worked. . We now have two little girls. My husband goes to sleep early, because he wakes up early in the morning for work. I usually try to work during the breakfast-lunch crowd. This allows me to get off early and have time together with him. He is a kind and gentle man and is very good with the girls.

Using the categories developed in the Dunedin study, Ellie would probably have been described as a reserved child. She remembers being told that she was shy when she was young and slow to warm up to new people and situations. While she became somewhat more confident around others as she entered school, as an adult, she still tends to be quiet and watch rather than interact with others in new situations.

Looking at the core response patterns from Chapter 3, Ellie would be described as having a weak sense of self-efficacy–she believed she lacked the ability to succeed in many areas of her life. It's easy to see from the above description of her childhood why this developed. Ellie struggled at school because she received little help or encouragement. The teasing from her brothers also made her believe that she wasn't as capable as others. All of this combined to make her reluctant to try new things or do her best.

Ellie developed an external locus of control because she was surrounded by parents and fellow students who blamed things outside of themselves for their problems. She simply adopted their way of viewing life.

Along with the ways of thinking that characterize a weak sense of self-efficacy and external locus of control were many unconscious conditioned emotional responses. These produced negative emotions when faced with challenges or difficulties. For example, while at school, whenever a test was announced, she would feel an immediate sense of dread along with thoughts about how she would probably not do well. This often resulted in her failing to study because she felt it was pointless, which caused poor performance.

As an adult, when faced with a new challenge, these conditioned emotional responses generated the same feelings of dread she felt when the teacher announced a test was to be given. Often, this caused her to avoid taking risks and feel like she had no power to make positive changes in her life.

The next chapter explores common forms of thinking that contribute to these types of negative response patterns and many of the negative emotions you experience. You'll also see how Ellie was able to change self-defeating response patterns that were limiting her life and develop new patterns that allowed her to experience life more fully.

SUMMARY OF KEY POINTS

- The Dunedin study identified five basic personality types that could first be clearly identified at the age of three and which were seen to persist into adulthood. They were labeled: confident, well-adjusted, reserved, inhibited, and undercontrolled.

- An increasing number of genes have been associated with specific traits. One striking example was the role that a gene known as MAOA plays in violent behavior. This gene has two forms: a short, weak form and a long, high-activity form. The weak form is common in adults who are violent criminals.

- About 30% of the population is now known to have the weak form of the MAOA gene that is common in adults who are violent criminals. However, most of them become productive members of society and lead normal lives. This means that, while you may have a genetic push in one direction or another, childhood plays a major role in shaping how that push is expressed.

- As an adult, you can make choices and learn to modify how you think and behave to soften the effects of both your genes and childhood background.

- Your childhood experiences create what will be called core response patterns. These are a collection of both unconscious conditioned emotional responses and conscious beliefs that generate many of the emotions you experience and cause you to react to others or the world in a specific way.

- Two examples of core response patterns are locus of control and self-efficacy.

  o Locus of control refers to how much control individuals believe they have over events and is used to determine why they succeeded or failed at something. The two categories that are usually described are internal and external locus of control.

  o Self-efficacy is the belief that individuals have concerning their ability to take actions that allow them to succeed in a particular situation.

- A genogram is a diagram of the main people in your life when you were growing up.

- Early recollections are a set of brief general descriptions of your experiences in grade school, middle school, high school, and early adulthood.

THINGS TO DO

- Recall what you were like as a child. If possible, ask your parents or other relatives what they think. Then, reread the descriptions for each of the Dunedin categories given at the beginning of the chapter and identify the one that best describes you.

o Confident

o Well-adjusted

o Reserved

o Undercontrolled

o Inhibited

- Think about the various areas of your life, such as family, work, school, and friends. Do any of the following statements reflect how you think about each area?

Outlook 1

o I often feel that I have little control over my life and what happens to me.

o People rarely get what they deserve.

o It isn't worth setting goals or making plans because too many things can happen that are outside of my control.

o Life is a game of chance.

o Individuals have little influence over the events of the world.

Outlook 2

o If you work hard and commit yourself to a goal, you can achieve anything.

o There is no such thing as fate or destiny.

o If you study hard and are well-prepared, you can do well on exams.

o Luck has little to do with success; it's mostly a matter of dedication and effort.

o In the long run, people tend to get what they deserve in life.

If any of the statements in Outlook 1 reflect your thinking in a particular area of your life, then you most likely have an external locus of control in this area.

If any of the statements in Outlook 2 reflect your outlook in an area of your life, then you most likely have an internal locus of control in that area. Keep in mind that you may have a strong locus of control in one area of your life and a weak locus of control in another.

- Now look at each of the areas of your life that you thought about in the previous exercise. Identify those where you believe that you have a strong ability to achieve success and reach your goals (a high sense of self-efficacy) and those where you believe you lack the ability to succeed and reach your goal (a low sense of self-efficacy). For example, a person might have a high level of confidence in their ability to do their job but have a low level of confidence in their ability to learn how to use a computer.

- Think about the adults who raised you along with what it was like in grade school, middle school, and high school. How have they influenced how you look at yourself, others, and the world around you? Some readers will find it useful to write their reflections. They can then use them when doing the recommended activities in the following chapters.

Chapter 5:

Habitual Thinking Patterns that Generate Negative Emotions

Until you make the unconscious conscious, it will direct your life and you will call it fate.

– C.G. Jung

This chapter begins with a look at a response pattern called "learned helplessness." It then explores the role that distorted thinking plays in producing many of the negative emotions you experience, along with ways to reduce the amount of distorted thinking you use.

LEARNED HELPLESSNESS

While American psychologist Martin Seligman was conducting research on classical conditioning in the late 1960s and early '70s, he discovered that when dogs received electric shocks from which there was no escape, they stopped trying to escape. This was true even later, when they were placed in a situation where escape or avoidance was possible.

At the same time, when dogs who had not received the previous shocks were placed in the same situation, they would take immediate action to escape. Seligman coined the term "learned helplessness" to describe this type of passivity that comes from the expectation that outcomes are uncontrollable.

Learned helplessness has since become a basic principle of behavioral theory and explains why individuals may accept and remain passive in negative situations despite their clear ability to change them. As a core response pattern, learned helplessness has both conscious thinking and unconscious conditioned emotional response patterns associated with it.

A sad but all too common example is children who have been severely abused. When children are mistreated and no one comes to their aid, they can be left feeling that nothing they do will change their situation. As adults, they can feel that they have no control over the difficulties they face and behave in a helpless manner. This can cause them to overlook opportunities for relief or change even when it is easily available. Learned helplessness in both children and adults is characterized by the following:

- Failure to ask for help
- Frustration
- Giving up
- Lack of effort
- Low self-esteem
- Passivity
- Poor motivation
- Procrastination

Core response patterns like learned helplessness–as well as those related to an external locus of control and weak sense of self-efficacy that were discussed in Chapter 4–have four basic parts:

- Beliefs
- Habitual thinking patterns that distort reality
- Habitual behaviors
- Subconscious conditioned emotional responses

All of these can generate depression, anger, or anxiety in the face of challenges.

INAPPROPRIATE EMOTIONS

An inappropriate emotion[8] is one that does not match the situation you are in. This might be an emotional response that is an illogical response to an event, or an emotional response that is more intense or muted than would normally be expected. While customs and behavior vary from culture to culture, in most Western cultures, becoming sad when hearing that a friend or relative has died is normal. Smiling and joking is not. Likewise, becoming irritated or disappointed when breaking a common everyday dish is a reasonable response. However, rage is not.

DISTORTED THINKING

Chapter 2 described some of the many things that your brain does that you are not aware of. It also described the brain's amazing ability to learn things so well that you don't have to think much about them as you do them. Getting dressed and doing routine work or

---

[8] The clinical term for an inappropriate emotional response is "inappropriate affect."

household chores were a few examples that were explored. It turns out that many of the thoughts you have are also learned habit patterns that you think without really being fully conscious of them. Because these automatic thinking patterns developed in childhood, some of the reasoning behind them is faulty. Since these types of patterns distort reality, you view events more negatively than they really are, or you fail to see important aspects of the events taking place around you.

Faulty habitual thinking patterns that distort your perception of events are called "distorted thinking"[9]. Since no one grows up in a perfect environment, everyone uses some of these types of thinking from time to time. This makes them a common source of the inappropriate emotions that each of us experiences. Thus, reducing the amount of distorted thinking you use helps you both experience fewer inappropriate emotions and respond more effectively to the various challenges that life presents. Unfortunately, one problem that arises when trying to change automatic behaviors, like distorted thinking, is the fact that you are mostly unaware of them.

Something I call the "new car principle"[10] can help you overcome this problem and become aware of when you are using self-talk associated with distorted thinking. This principle refers to the way your brain identifies the things you spend time and energy on as important. It then causes you to notice them whenever they are present. It takes

---

[9] The types of distorted thinking described in this book are also referred to as cognitive distortions or heuristics.

[10] The "new car principle" is based on cognitive biases that go by the names of frequency illusion, Baader-Meinhof phenomenon, and recency illusion.

its name from the experience that people often have after buying a new car. Suddenly, you notice cars of the same model as yours wherever you go. It's as if hundreds of them are everywhere, when prior to your purchase there seemed to be none. They were always there – you simply didn't notice them. Because you put so much time, thought, and effort into selecting this particular car, your mind has identified it as important. So, it now notices this type of car wherever you go. The same thing happens whenever you put time and energy into something. The deeper part of your brain identifies it as important and causes you to notice things around you associated with it.

Memorizing the words or phrases associated with the various types of distorted thinking can help you notice when you are using them. However, becoming aware of your distorted thinking is just the first step. To change how you think and the inappropriate emotions generated by distorted thinking, you need to replace distorted thinking with logical and rational thoughts. These new thoughts are called "rational challenges."

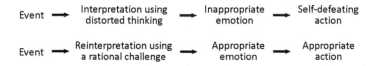

Like many habits, habitual thinking is mostly automatic and unconscious. Thus, it takes time to change deeply ingrained patterns of negative thoughts. However, as you practice doing this, the new thoughts begin to replace the old thoughts and become more and more the way you think.

THE RECURRENCE OF OLD PATTERNS

One thing that sometimes causes distress is the fact that old patterns tend to recur when you are sick, tired, or experiencing unusual stress. When this happens, don't be alarmed or feel that your efforts have been in vain. This is usually just a message that you need to take care of yourself. It's especially important for people who tend to ignore their needs and the effect that stress might have on them. Once you've taken time for self-care, you'll see the former progress you've made return.

The best way to use rational challenges is to memorize statements that point out the flaw in the specific types of distorted thinking you use. This helps you reinterpret events in a more logical and rational manner. Both this and the next chapter give examples of effective rational challenges for each of the forms of distorted thinking described. We'll start with challenges that Ellie, whose profile is in Chapter 4, used for four common types of distorted thinking that were part of her habitual self-talk: all-or-nothing thinking, overgeneralization, magnification, and minimization.

ALL-OR-NOTHING THINKING

All-or-nothing thinking[11] views the world in absolute terms. Events are always black or white, everything or nothing, good or bad, success or failure. This type of absolute thinking makes it difficult to celebrate small successes and learn from mistakes.

This was especially typical of Ellie's thoughts and behavior when going to school. When she had difficulty with a subject, she would

---

[11] All-or-nothing thinking is also known as dichotomous thinking, black and white thinking, and polarized thinking.

give up and tell herself, "I'll never be able to do well." This would happen even when she had made significant progress. A mistake or difficulty caused her to see her entire effort as a failure. This type of thinking continued after graduating.

When a new upscale restaurant opened close by, she went in to see if she could work there. After the interview with the manager, she left thinking about one moment when she had difficulty responding to a question. This caused her to think of the entire interview as a failure, even though there was just this one small stumble. She even remembered being amazed that they hired her. She reasoned that it must be because there were so few people seeking work at that time, not because she was skilled as a waitress and did well during the interview.

The most effective way to challenge an all-or-nothing thought is to question its absolute nature. Ask yourself, "Is this event really so 'wrong' or 'bad'?" Then, find examples from your own experience that contradict the black-and-white categories you have created. You might even be able to find some positive aspects of the event.

After learning about all-or-nothing thinking, Ellie recalled what she was thinking after the interview:

> "He asked about how my experience would fit in with that type of restaurant, and it took me time to think of an answer. The whole interview was awful."

In order to practice creating rational challenges, Ellie came up with the following:

> "I was using all-or-nothing thinking. My small stumble did not cancel out everything else I said. My experience allowed

me to understand and respond to all of his other questions well. After I had a moment to think about it, I even came up with an OK answer to the one I stumbled on. In the big picture, one small misstep is usually not important. The proof of this is that I got the job!"

Overgeneralizing

When you overgeneralize, you take a single negative event and turn it into a never-ending pattern of defeat or misfortune. Words like "always," "never," "everything," and "nothing" are common in self-talk when overgeneralizing.

- Why does this always happen to me?
- Things never seem to work out the way I want them to!
- Every time I try to be nice, I get burned!

When you notice yourself overgeneralizing, challenge the extreme nature of your statement with questions such as:

- Is this really true?
- Do things never work out?
- Does this actually happen every time?

Often, it helps to recall one or more incidents that directly contradict the negative overgeneralization.

It's common for all-or-nothing thinking to include overgeneralizations. This was true for Ellie, who noticed that her all-or-nothing thinking after the interview also included the thoughts:

"I always blow it when I interview. I'm never going to get a job."

Recalling her thoughts, she created the following rational challenge:

"Wait, a minute. I was not only doing all-or-nothing thinking; I was also overgeneralizing. I don't always blow it. I got my last job and I'll get another, even if it's not this one."

When Ellie first recalled what she had been thinking after the interview, she felt some of the negative feelings she experienced. However, as she practiced challenging the distorted thinking that she had used, she noticed a sense of calm confidence that was new to her. This is because she had *reinterpreted* events more realistically.

Magnification

Magnification – sometimes called catastrophic thinking or catastrophizing – is a very common type of distorted thinking. It refers to the exaggeration of minor flaws or problems, so they seem worse than they are. While there are many ways in which people exaggerate the seriousness of events, words like "terrible," "awful," and "horrible" are often used.

Ellie had the habit of magnifying the significance of minor mistakes. While putting together side dishes for an order at work, she would sometimes spill or drop something. She would then both magnify and overgeneralize:

"This is terrible. Why does this always happen when I'm busy?"

Later, when thinking about her thoughts, she identified what she had done and used a rational challenge to counter her thoughts:

"What happened was not terrible. It was just a normal occurrence in a busy restaurant. It also doesn't always happen when I'm busy. I'm usually pretty good at handling lots of things at the same time. This is just an occasional occurrence."

As with the previous all-or-nothing example, Ellie's taking time to challenge distorted thinking at a later time illustrates an important practice. You are often too busy taking care of events that are occurring around you to be aware of your negative self-talk. Taking time later to review what you were thinking during times when you were upset can help you identify distorted thinking that you use and develop rational challenges. With time, this helps to make you aware of your distorted thinking when it is occurring. The challenges you developed while calm will also come to mind.

Ellie found this to be true. After a few weeks of reviewing her thoughts when she was at home, another spill occurred. As in the past, her first impulse was to magnify the spill into a major tragedy. However, just as quickly, she noticed what she was doing and thought:

> "There's that old thinking again. This isn't terrible. It's just something that's part of the job and happens now and then. Now, clean it up and get back to work. You're doing good."

After challenging her distorted thinking, Ellie was pleased at how calm she felt. In the past, a minor mishap like this would cause Ellie to be upset for some time afterwards.

In addition to the words already mentioned, there are two common phrases that reflect magnification, "I can't stand it" and "I can't take it." People will use these phrases to describe their reaction to minor things that are really just unpleasant. For example, while driving to work, an accident had backed up traffic. Ellie became angry and thought:

> "Look at this! I can't take the traffic in this town anymore."

Because of the work she had been doing with self-talk, she noticed this and challenged it with:

> "What am I saying? The traffic is not killing me or causing me to lose anything. It's just an obnoxious part of living in this town. The truth is, I can and do take it often. I just don't like it. Now, relax and enjoy some music."

She was pleasantly surprised at how reinterpreting events calmed her down.

Minimization

Minimization–also called discounting–involves ignoring or invalidating good things that have happened to you. Minimizing undermines your faith in your abilities and contributes to a weak sense of self-efficacy that was described in Chapter 4. Rather than recognizing your strengths, you assume you aren't competent or skilled. When positive things happen, they are not the result of anything you have done. You just got lucky. For example, when Ellie was chosen as employee of the month, rather than feeling proud of her achievement, her first thought was:

> "I guess they ran out of people to choose for this and were stuck with me."

Having just read about minimization, she noticed what she was thinking and challenged this with:

> "Wait, a minute. This is what I used to do in school when I did well on a test and would think I just got lucky. They chose me because I'm a good worker and they honestly wanted to let me know."

As she reinterpreted the meaning of the award, Ellie's mood shifted from feeling embarrassed and slightly ashamed to feeling a sense of pride and satisfaction. While this was a somewhat new feeling for her in situations like this, she liked it. It felt good.

The next chapter looks at three additional forms of distorted thinking that are common, along with core response patterns that are often associated with them.

SUMMARY OF KEY POINTS

- Learned helplessness occurs when an individual continuously faces a negative, uncontrollable situation and stops trying to change their circumstances, even when they later have the ability to do so.

- An inappropriate emotion is one that is an illogical response to an event or an emotional response that is more intense or muted than expected.

- Distorted thinking is a term used to describe habitual thinking patterns that leads you to view yourself and events more negatively than they really are.

- The new car principle refers to how your brain uses the things you spend time and energy on as a guide to select what you become consciously aware of.

- Self-talk refers to thoughts that take the form of silent conversations you have in your mind.

- Rational challenges are responses used to challenge distorted thinking with logical and rational thoughts.

- After making progress in replacing distorted thinking with rational challenges, old patterns will sometimes return when you are sick, tired, or experiencing unusual stress. The recurrence of old patterns is usually just a message that you need to take care of yourself.

- All-or-nothing thinking views the world in absolute terms. Events are always black or white, everything or nothing, good or bad, success or failure. It is best challenged by questioning the absolute nature of it. Ask yourself, "Is this event really so 'wrong' or 'bad'?" Then, find examples from your own experience that contradict the black-and-white categories you have created.

- Overgeneralizing is taking a single negative event and turning it into a never-ending pattern of defeat or misfortune. Words like "always," "never," "everything," and "nothing" are common in self-talk when overgeneralizing. Challenge it by questioning the extreme nature of your thoughts.

- Magnification is the exaggeration of minor flaws or problems, so they seem worse than they actually are.

- Minimization involves ignoring or invalidating the good things that have happened to you.

THINGS TO DO

- Are there any difficult situations you face where you have given up on trying to make things better? If so, reexam them and identify any positive steps you can take. Sometimes it helps to talk about situations like this with a person you trust.

- Take ten to fifteen minutes each day to think about times when you became upset. Recall the things you thought or said to yourself. Did any of it match the forms of distorted thinking described in this chapter? If so, use the next activity to become more aware of your distorted thinking and challenge it.

- Create a rational challenge for each type of distorted thinking you identify. While this can be done by simply reflecting on the day and thinking of rational challenges in your mind, many find it even more effective to write their thoughts down. The reason for this is that writing things down utilizes the new car principle discussed in this chapter. It alerts the deeper part of your mind that this type of work is important. As you practice identifying distorted thinking and creating rational challenges, you will begin noticing your distorted thinking more often when you are actually using it. Because you've thought about it beforehand, you will also have well thought out challenges you can use that fit your personality.

- While some like to use a journal to record their thoughts and challenges, others like to use a computer. Many find it useful to put challenges for the specific types of distorted thinking they frequently use on Rational Thought Cards. These can then be posted in places where you will see them during the day. Use whichever of these ideas that best fits your personality and lifestyle.

Reviewing rational challenges you've created makes them easy to recall when you're upset and helps you view events in a more realistic way. Reinterpreting events in this manner helps quiet any inappropriate emotions that you are feeling.

Here are cards that Ellie made when working on the types of distorted thinking discussed in this chapter. Yours may be different. The important thing is to create rational challenges that fit your situation and personality.

Ellie carried her Rational Thought Cards in her purse and read them two or three times each day for a week. It surprised her how often she used this type of thinking. She was also pleased at how her rational challenges helped to both calm her and enable her to focus on finding solutions instead of being upset.

ALL-OR-NOTHING THINKING

What's Happening
When I was young, I was on my own and often faced obstacles that were too big for a child to face alone. As a result, I learned to give up and say things like, "This is hopeless" or "I'll never get this."

What's Real
I'm an intelligent and capable woman. As an adult, I can now do much more than I thought I could do when I was young. I am learning to recognize and challenge my old all-or-nothing thinking and face problems with patience and courage.

Positive Shift
Things are rarely all or nothing or black and white. I am able to calmly look for solutions and ask for help when I need it. I also recognize that learning new things means there will be times when it's difficult. I can take a break, and then try again. I can do it.

OVERGENERALIZING

What's Happening

When I was young I copied my parents' behavior and learned to turn small negative events into a never-ending pattern of defeat or misfortune. Like them, I would say things like, "Why does this always happen to me?," "Nothing ever goes the way I want it to," and "I'll never get this."

What's Real

When I say things like this, I'm usually just facing a minor inconvenience or a problem that has a solution. I am also becoming more aware of my ability to solve the various problems I encounter. I can also see that even when there are difficulties, things usually work out well.

Positive Shift

"Always" and "never" are rarely true. Now, recall the many times I've found great solutions and been successful. This is just a problem to be solved, and I can do it.

MAGNIFICATION

What's Happening

When my parents encountered small problems, they would exaggerate them by saying how "terrible" or "awful" they were. My mom would often say "I can't stand it" when she was finding something difficult. I learned to do the same thing.

What's Real

Most things are not terrible or awful. They are usually just a momentary inconvenience. I have also dealt with many adversities in my life successfully. While I may sometimes bend a little, I don't break.

Positive Shift

This problem is not a big deal. I am a strong and capable adult. Now, let's find a solution.

MINIMIZATION

What's Happening

My parents tended to be very critical and only rarely encouraged me. Because of this and the frequent put-downs by my brothers, I thought I was dumb and not very capable. This caused me to feel self-conscious and worthless. So, I would minimize any compliment I received or nice thing that happened.

What's Real

The negative self-image I developed as a child was a lie. The truth is that I am an able adult who has the same value as everyone else.

Positive Shift

Enjoy the positive feelings that come with healthy relationships. Be pleased with my abilities and achievements. Just say, "Thank you," when given a compliment.

Chapter 6:

Two Additional Forms of Distorted Thinking

Thinking something does not make it true.
Wanting something does not make it real.

– Michelle Hodkin

Chapter 5 discussed three common forms of distorted thinking, along with ways to challenge them. This chapter continues the discussion by focusing on two additional forms of distorted thinking: should/must thinking and circular why questioning. The chapter begins with Sharon's profile to illustrate how distorted thinking can even develop in what most would describe as a positive childhood.

SHARON

As with Ellie in Chapter 4, Sharon's genogram provides a picture of the family she grew up in. It has one new feature: the zigzag line between her mother and father. This shows that they divorced when she was ten. Her mother married again when she was nineteen. Her father married another woman with a son from a previous relationship. Since Sharon rarely saw her stepmother's former husband, he was left out of the genogram and Sharon's early recollections. As with Ellie, Sharon's genogram is followed by descriptions of the adults in her life and early recollections.

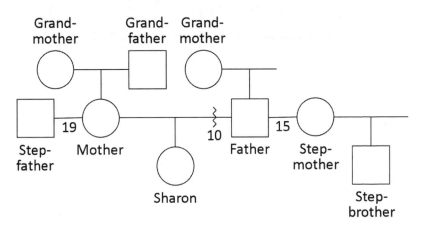

Grand-mother Grand-father Grand-mother

19 Step-father Mother

10 15 Father Step-mother

Sharon

Step-brother

Mother

Mom was a teacher at a local, state-run two-year college that prepared students to go on to a four-year college or university. She was smart and very involved in my life. We were very close, both when I was young and now. She was very encouraging and a good listener; however, she always had high expectations for me and could be very picky about how things were done.

Father

Father was a supervisor at a local factory. He was a confident man who knew what he wanted. While he was very assertive, he could also be very gentle and loving. He had participated in sports while in school and loved to watch all kinds of sporting events on television. He enjoyed playing on local softball and basketball teams.

Grandmother (Mother's Mom)

Grandmother was kind, gentle, and fun to be with. She was a grade-school teacher when she was younger.

Grandfather (Mother's Dad)

Grandfather always had a joke or something funny to say. He had been in the army and became a firefighter. He had lots of stories and enjoyed talking about the things I was doing.

Grandmother (Father's Mom)

My father's mother was a somewhat reserved person. However, she enjoyed playing games and talking about her life as a nurse. When I was young and visited her, we would play cards, board games, or do fun things like baking cookies.

Grandfather (Father's Dad)

My father's dad died when I was young, so I don't remember him.

Stepfather (Mother's Second Husband)

After the divorce, Mom married a man who also taught at the college where she worked. He was outgoing and enjoyed talking about the things going on in the world. Since I was nineteen when they married, we interacted more like two adults than as parent and child.

Stepmother (Father's Second Wife)

My father married a woman who was an administrator in the fire district where he worked. While she was often quiet, she was friendly and enjoyed going to concerts, movies, and sporting events. We mainly interacted when I was with my dad, so my stepmother and I were never very close.

Stepbrother

I would see my stepbrother occasionally; he was older and involved with computer programming. He was friendly, but we had little in common.

EARLY RECOLLECTIONS

Childhood through Grade School

I did well in grade school. Mom and Dad were always there to help with homework and any school project I was doing. We were always going someplace, such as a movie, a local park for a picnic, or a family vacation.

Outside of school, I was involved with different types of activities, such as swimming, dancing, and martial arts. Mom seemed to always be there, and I loved it all. She always encouraged me to do my best.

As middle school approached, I could see tension between my parents. However, they tried to keep their problems private. Still, I noticed the distance between them, so it wasn't a surprise when they told me they were going to separate. Looking back, I can see that they both worked very hard to help me understand that their problems had nothing to do with me and they still loved me.

Middle School

I continued to do well in school and found myself at the top of the class in most of my subjects. Mom and Dad were now divorced. I lived with Mom but saw Dad almost every week for a day or so. Mom continued to keep me busy with activities. When I was with Dad, we would go someplace and have a great time together. Often, his new wife would stay home, so it would be just the two of us. During these times I was truly Daddy's little girl.

High School

The routine with Mom and Dad was now a regular thing. While they had separate lives, I was still a big part of each of their lives. They would both be at important events, such as a birthday or performance.

I was in advanced classes at school. Since many of the same kids were in each of my classes, I developed several close friends. Some continued after high school. During the first two years, I was involved in basketball, but a foot injury sidelined me for the rest of high school.

Early Adult

After graduating from high school, I went on to college and received a BA and then an MA. I began teaching at the same college where Mom had been working and enjoyed it thoroughly. I met a wonderful man there, and we now have two children, a boy and a girl.

Sharon presents quite a contrast to Ellie. Looking at the interaction of their predispositions and the environment in which they grew up, it's easy to see why. Sharon was a well-adjusted child while Ellie was a reserved child.[12]

Sharon's parents allowed her to make many different types of decisions for herself. This resulted in an internal locus of control where she felt she was in charge of her life and responsible for whether she succeeded or failed at the things she tried. Ellie grew up in a home and social environment where there were few opportunities to try new things and most decisions were made for her. This resulted in an external locus of control where she felt she had little control over the events that influenced her life.

Sharon's natural self-confidence and openness to new experiences, along with her parent's encouragement and the success she had, in school and outside activities, gave her a strong sense of self-efficacy. In contrast, Ellie's lack of support and encouragement at home resulted in poor achievement at school. This, along with her reserved nature, produced a lack of self-confidence and a weak sense of self-efficacy.

While Ellie faced many disadvantages while growing up, most would see Sharon as having a basically good childhood. They would also see her as being a well-adjusted and successful adult.

TWO ADDITIONAL FORMS OF DISTORTED THINKING

Like all of us, Sharon would occasionally experience inappropriate emotions. However, unlike Ellie, this was because of two different, but very common, forms of distorted thinking known as should/must thinking and circular why questioning.

---

[12] See Chapter 4 for the discussions on the five basic personality types that were identified in the babies by the Dunedin Study and the ideas of locus of control and self-efficacy.

Should/Must Thinking

It's perfectly logical and correct to use words like "should," "must," and "have to" when an outcome depends on a certain action. For example, "I have to leave by 7 if I want to arrive by 8." In contrast to this type of rational thought is the form of distorted thinking called should/must thinking.

Should/must thinking involves thoughts or statements that use the words "should," "must," "have to," or "can't" to transform a preference or desire into a rigid rule. For example, one of Sharon's rules was, "You should always be on time." While this is a useful rule in many situations, should/must thinking caused this to be an unbreakable rule for Sharon. When a rigid rule like this is broken or when the desired outcome is not met, it causes an exaggerated emotional response and the self-defeating behavior of becoming problem focused. You not only become upset, but you also focus on how awful the situation is rather than considering what you can do to make things better.

The key to changing should/must thinking is to realize there is nothing you *have* to do in life. People often object when I say this and respond with statements such as "I have to go to work!" When I respond by telling them, "No, you don't have to go to work," they usually give various reasons for why they "have" to go to work. After listening to their reasons, I point out that they are choosing to go to work because they either want to obtain something positive or avoid a negative consequence. The bottom line is that life is a series of *choices* that we make based on what we think will help us gain the things we want and avoid the things we don't want.

Like most of our behavior, many of the rules adults have were taught to them during childhood. Some were meant to help them avoid danger, such as "Look both ways before crossing the street." Others helped them in social settings, such as "Always say 'please' and 'thank you.'" One of the developmental tasks of adulthood is to reexamine the rules we learned in childhood and see if they are still valid.

One way to do this is to notice times when you use words like "should," "must," "have to," or "can't." Whenever you find yourself talking or thinking like this, substitute the phrases "I like," "I want," or "I prefer." For example, when Sharon got caught in heavy traffic that was going to make her late for a social gathering, she would say or think:

"Oh no, this can't be happening. I can't be late."

It would be more accurate for Sharon to say or think:

"I like to be on time."

"I want to be on time."

"I prefer to be on time."

While Sharon wants to be on time, she doesn't *have* to be on time. While it's often important to be on time to achieve something you want, there is no cosmic rule that says you always have to be on time.

After learning about should/must thinking, Sharon was once again caught in heavy traffic and began to think the same old automatic thoughts of, "I can't be late. I have to make it there on time." She caught herself and challenged her thoughts with:

"While I very much like to be on time, I don't have to be on time. It's not like anything tragic will happen if I show up a little late to my friend's house, and with this traffic, I'm probably going to be a little late. There is nothing I can do about it. So just relax and get there when you can. I can call and let them know I'll be a little late. Now, relax and listen to some music. Do your best, and just get there when you get there."

While Sharon became much calmer, she was still a little anxious. The excessive anxiety associated with being late was a conditioned emotional response and was going to take time to change. However, she was pleased that she was much more relaxed than she normally was in this type of situation. She could also think about the upcoming time with her friend rather than becoming obsessed with the traffic. In the past, as her anxiety increased, she would drive in an unsafe manner as she tried to make up time.

Another benefit that people experience as they gain skill in noticing and challenging should/must thinking is that they feel more in control of their life. The locus of control is outside of you in areas of your life dominated by should/must thinking. It often feels like an invisible parent is making you do things rather than you deciding for yourself what you want to do. Using the language of choice and substituting "want," "like," or "prefer" for your "shoulds" and "musts" allows you to gain control over when you think your rules are beneficial and when they can be disregarded. You become the one deciding what is best for you. This also helps you deal with situations where you do not get what you want more realistically.

While everyone does at least some should/must thinking, the rules for people who grew up in harsh environments are more rigid than those of people who grew up in safer and more nurturing environments. This is because their rigid should/must rules often serve to help them reduce or avoid physical and emotional pain. For example, children in an abusive home may have the rule, "never make waves," because breaking the rule resulted in physical or emotional abuse. Unfortunately, this rule is often carried into adulthood.

Circular Why Questioning

While should/must thinking is easy to spot, there is a related form of distorted thinking I call "circular why questioning"[13] that is harder to see in oneself. Circular why questioning is the act of asking a series of questions over and over with no actual attempt to answer them. Often, when asked, a person gives a perfectly reasonable answer. On their own, they just never think of it.

When you watch people using circular why questioning, it appears as though they have "short-circuited" in some fashion. However, their apparent confusion is because of the difficulty they are having in accepting the fact that reality is not conforming to one or more of their beliefs about how the world "should" be.

Circular why questioning usually involves thoughts or statements with "why" or "how." For example, a person who has done something that they regretted later may dwell on the misbehavior and think:

---

[13] This is a term I use to describe a form of distorted thinking that I have seen with clients, but which is not found in most lists of distorted thinking. It is not to be confused with how some family therapies use the term "circular questioning."

"Why did I do that? I don't understand how I could have acted that way."

An effective way to challenge circular why questioning is to:

- Answer the question
- Identify the should/must rule that is being violated
- Challenge the should/must rule

Here is an example of circular why questioning that Sharon engaged in after giving a presentation to fellow instructors. As she ended her presentation, she forgot to conclude with a point that she had thought was important while preparing. Later she thought over and over:

> "I don't understand how I totally forgot about that and blew it. Why wasn't I able to see what I had clearly written on my notes? That was so stupid!"

Later, as Sharon reflected on how upset she had become, she noticed her circular why questioning and wrote the following challenge:

Answer the Question
I didn't make the point that was on my outline because I was running out of time and distracted by a question just before closing that took more time to answer than I had expected.

What Should/Must Rule Was Violated?
My circular why questioning came from that old core response that mistakes are unacceptable, and I need to do things perfectly.

Challenge the Should/Must Rule

There is no such thing as perfection with people. I made a small omission. After all was said and done, it wasn't really important. The presentation went well, and I received excellent evaluations from the teachers who were there. Several said how helpful it had been. The omission didn't really detract from the presentation at all. Be pleased with how well you did!

The next chapter explores core response patterns that are often associated with the types of distorted thinking described in both this chapter and Chapter 5.

SUMMARY OF KEY POINTS

- Should/must thinking is a form of distorted thinking that makes rigid rules for something that is only a preference or desire.

- The locus of control becomes external in areas of your life dominated by should/must thinking.

- Challenge should/must thinking by substituting the phrases "I should" and "I must" with "I like," "I want," or "I prefer."

- Life is a series of choices that we make based on what we think will help us gain the things we want and avoid the things we don't want.

- People who grew up in harsh environments tend to have should/must rules that are more rigid than those of people who grew up in safe and nurturing environments.

- Circular why questioning is the act of asking a series of questions over and over with no actual attempt to answer them. They usually have the words "why" or "how."

- An effective way to challenge circular why questioning is to:
  o Answer the question
  o Identify the should/must rule that is being violated
  o Challenge the should/must rule

THINGS TO DO

- Recall times when you've been upset and identify any should/must thinking or circular why questioning you were using. If you identify any, create a rational challenge for it.

- Take some time to identify the various should/must rules you follow in daily life. For each one, answer the following:
  o Is this something I was taught when young?
  o Is this something I came up with on my own?
  o If it's something I came up with on my own, why was it important to create this rule?

  After you've answered the above questions, decide:
  o Do I want to keep this rule just as it is?
  o Do I want to change this rule in some way?
  o Do I want to discard it and stop following this rule?

- Create cards with ideas you can use to challenge should/must thinking and circular why questioning. Here are two examples of cards that Sharon created. When creating your own cards, use ideas that fit your situation and personality.

SHOULD/MUST THINKING

What's Happening

When things don't go the way I want them to, I sometimes begin to dwell on how things "should" have happened or what I "should" have done.

What's Real

There are some things that I have little control over. Because I'm human, I sometimes make mistakes. When appropriate, identify where the rule behind my should/must thinking came from; often it's from Mom.

Positive Shift

Change my thoughts by saying "I would have liked or wanted things to be a certain way, but they aren't." Become proactive and focus on a solution. What action can I take to deal with the situation or possibly make things better? I can also decide if the rule behind my should/must thinking is something I want to keep, discard, or change.

CIRCULAR WHY QUESTIONING

What's Happening

When something bad happens or I make a mistake, I sometimes find myself asking, "Why did this happen?" or "Why did I do this?" rather than looking for a solution.

What's Real

When this happens, I know the answer to my questions. Usually, I just don't like the answer. Often, there's a should/must rule that has been violated.

Positive Shift

I'm learning to become more of a positive realist. I can accept that the world and the events that take place are what they are. While they are often not what I want, I can acknowledge that I would have liked things to be different. I can then focus on finding a solution that takes care of my needs.

Chapter 7:

A Closer Look at Core Response Patterns

Yes, beliefs are important for they shape who we are, but our identity is revealed not through our beliefs or our talk, but through our actions.

−Thomas Ingram

Chapters 4 and 5 describe three well-researched core response patterns that have simple labels: locus of control, self-efficacy, and learned helplessness. This chapter explores other types of core response patterns, along with ways to change those that cause inappropriate emotions that are too intense or an illogical response for what would normally be expected.

LABELS FOR CORE RESPONSE PATTERNS

Over the past century, different approaches have been used to identify the various core response patterns that people have. In the 1930s, Frederic Bartlett used the term "schema" (skee-muh) as part of his research into how memory works. Jean Piaget expanded the idea of schemas in his theories on the cognitive development of children. In the 1970s and '80's schemas came to represent broad concepts in one's memory for objects, oneself, people, events, one's culture, and one's role in life. For example, Jeffrey Young has described what he calls early maladaptive schemas.

Alfred Adler, another well-known psychologist in the early twentieth century, used the term "lifestyle" to describe how people react to others and social situations. His work influenced Eric Berne, who coined the term "life scripts" as part of his development of transactional analysis in the 1960s and '70s.

These attempts to describe core response patterns have two things in common. First, they all used simple phrases or sentences to describe the core response patterns they identified. Adler used phrases such as "ruling type" and "socially useful type." Eric Berne used short sentences such as "I'm not okay, You're okay." Psychologists such as Jeffrey Young used labels such as "defectiveness/shame" and "dependence/incompetence." Second, they saw that core response patterns develop during childhood and are shaped by a combination of the genetic predisposition of a child, the influence of the adults who are raising the child, and the child's social and family environment.

The last two chapters discussed how the use of labels to identify the automatic thought patterns called distorted thinking helps you become fully conscious of them. Being aware of what you are thinking allows you to practice substituting more rational thoughts. As you do this, the new thoughts slowly replace the old patterns. In the same way, creating labels for core response patterns that generate disruptive emotions and self-defeating behaviors helps you become fully conscious of them. This allows you to substitute a more appropriate response.

When creating a label for a response pattern, it's useful to think of the saying, "If it looks like a duck, talks like a duck, and walks like a duck, it's probably a duck." Applying this idea to core response patterns, we can say, "If you act as if you have a particular core response pattern, speak as if you have a particular core response pattern, and think as if you have a particular core response pattern, this pattern accurately describes associations behind some of your emotions and behavior."

Because every person has a unique childhood experience, they see the world differently. We could fill pages listing all of the possible labels for positive and negative core response patterns people have. However, labels for some of the mosre common patterns are listed in the following list. They are divided into three broad categories: how you see yourself, how you see others, and how you see the world.

Since no one has a perfect childhood, we all have a combination of patterns that generate inappropriate emotions and self-defeating behaviors along with those that generate appropriate emotions and behaviors that help us succeed in life. So, an opposite positive pattern is given for each negative pattern. As you read through the list, put a check by any that describes how you react to the various situations in your life.

EXAMPLES OF CORE RESPONSE PATTERNS CONCERNING TO YOURSELF

Negative	Positive
I'm not as capable as others	I am as capable as others
I'm worthless	I have the same value as anyone else
I'm unlovable/unlikable	I am lovable/likable
I'm dirty/ugly/bad	I am fine just as I am

Emotions/anger is dangerous	I can manage my emotions/anger effectively
Never show any sign of weakness	There are times when it's appropriate to show my vulnerabilities and weaknesses
Never do anything that makes you look stupid or ignorant	Making mistakes and doing something silly doesn't matter to people who are kind and reasonable
I must always be strong	There are times when it's okay to show weakness
Mistakes are unacceptable	Mistakes happen and most are not that important
Negative	Positive
I'm not as capable as others	I am as capable as others
I'm worthless	I have the same value as anyone else
I'm unlovable/unlikable	I am lovable/likable
I'm dirty/ugly/bad	I am fine just as I am
Emotions/anger is dangerous	I can manage my emotions/anger effectively
Never show any sign of weakness	There are times when it's appropriate to show my vulnerabilities and weaknesses
Never do anything that makes you look stupid or ignorant	Making mistakes and doing something silly doesn't matter to people who are kind and reasonable
I must always be strong	There are times when it's okay to show weakness
Mistakes are unacceptable	Mistakes happen and most are not that important

EXAMPLES OF CORE RESPONSE PATTERNS CONCERNING OTHERS

Negative	Positive
Intimacy is painful/dangerous	Intimacy is important and, with the right people, satisfies a deep part of me
Conflict is dangerous	I am able to resolve conflicts with others in a satisfying way
I'm responsible for how others feel	People are responsible for their own emotions
People always leave me	I can have long-lasting relationships
People always let you down	I have people who are there for me in both good and bad times
You can't trust anyone	There are people you can trust
You can't trust the opposite sex	There are members of the opposite sex who are trustworthy
Never do anything that hurts others	People sometimes react poorly for reasons that have nothing to do with me
Never let any slight or wrong go unpunished	There are times when I need to be gracious and forgive others

EXAMPLES OF CORE RESPONSE PATTERNS CONCERNING THE WORLD

Negative	Positive
I can't win at anything	I am able to achieve important goals and succeed when I put my mind to it
The world is fearful and dangerous	I can find safety and manage threats
Life is meaningless	I can find meaning in life

I have no power or control	I am able to deal with the uncertainties of life
I need to be in control of the various aspects of my life	I can accept that there are some things in life that you have no control over
Winning is everything	While I like to win, losing does not make me less of a person

As you read through the above list, you probably identified some labels as describing both positive and negative ways in which you generally react. Now, look at the list again and think about how you react in intimate settings with loved ones, with people at work, and with people you don't know in public places. It's common to have a response pattern that is only seen in one of these settings. This is especially true for patterns you have in intimate settings.

Because patterns associated with intimacy developed when you were young, they are often only triggered in an intimate setting. Those associated with work and other adult activities usually develop when you are older and may only be triggered in those settings.

IDENTIFYING PROBLEM RESPONSE PATTERNS

As Sharon looked through the list, the phrase "mistakes are unacceptable" leaped out at her. As she read the words, the challenges she had written in response to her should/must thinking came to mind.[14] She could also recall several recent times when she became overly upset about mistakes she had made. As she considered what her behavior would look like if she saw it in someone else, she thought, "I'm behaving as if perfection is actually possible."

---

[14] See the discussions on should/must thinking and circular why questioning in Chapter 6.

Now, if you asked Sharon if she thought it was possible to always do things so they were perfect with no flaws, she would say, "No." She would readily admit that mistakes are a normal part of life and wanting to always do things perfectly is unreasonable. However, her behavior and emotional response to mistakes and imperfection said these response patterns were a deeply embedded part of her automatic thoughts and the conditioned emotional responses connected to them.

Like many core response patterns, Sharon's had several sources. As a child, she showed a tendency to be meticulous in how she approached life. This inborn genetic tendency was exaggerated by Sharon's mother, who modeled perfectionistic behavior and self-talk that Sharon simply copied. As she thought about it, Sharon identified many of the phrases she said when she made a mistake as being the same as the ones that her mother uses.

Another source of Sharon's perfectionism was her mother's reaction whenever she did poorly at something. While Sharon's mother could be very gracious with her students at school, she had high expectations and hopes for her daughter. This, along with her own perfectionism, caused her to point out whenever Sharon made a mistake. While she did this in a kind way, it still made Sharon very aware of when she didn't smeasure up to her mother's expectations.

One incident that Sharon recalled was a time in grade school when she received a mark of "needs improvement" in one of her subjects. While her mother said, "That's okay. We'll work on that for next time," Sharon remembered the disappointed look on her mother's face. Like most children, Sharon wanted to please her mother. Countless experiences like this gave Sharon the message that mistakes are intolerable and exaggerated her need to do things perfectly so her mother would be pleased.

Something else that helped reinforce the conditioned emotional responses associated with Sharon's perfectionism was the fact that humans, like other mammals, have an amazing ability to read the body language and expressions of others. We are born with this ability, and it's what often gives us intuitions about others. Like all abilities, it is stronger in some than in others and can be enhanced or diminished by one's early childhood experiences.

Here is a simple activity that demonstrates this ability. Say the phrase, "I love you" as a question. Now say it as a casual greeting to a friend. Now say it tenderly, as if to someone you love deeply. The tone in your voice and the expressions on your face automatically vary each time. You would also instantly understand the underlying meaning if someone said this simple phrase to you in each of these three ways.

Babies and young children are especially aware of the subtle messages that your expression, tone of voice, and body language provide. So, even though Sharon's mother tried to be encouraging, her nonverbal language revealed her disappointment when Sharon made a mistake or didn't quite hit the mark at a task. So, after a childhood filled with hundreds, if not thousands, of experiences like this, Sharon developed a deeply embedded conditioned emotional response associated with mistakes and imperfection.

Before we explore how to change a pattern like this, consider what the opposite of perfectionism would be: having no concern for mistakes or how well or poorly something is done. These two patterns, perfectionism and disregard for results, are at opposite ends of a continuum. The middle between them would be a response that reflected a desire to do things well but accepted minor flaws and shortcomings. This can be diagrammed as:

No concern for mistakes or how well or how poorly a task is done	━━	Desire to do things well but OK with minor flaws or shortcomings	━━	Mistakes are unacceptable and anything short of perfection is intolerable

While extreme perfectionism can paralyze a person, it turns out that a little perfectionism can make a person very successful in life. This was certainly true for Sharon. So, when you identify a response pattern that is causing problems, take a moment to consider what the opposite pattern would be and how it would influence your life. Often, you may find that what you've identified as a negative response pattern is just an exaggeration of what is generally a positive pattern.

This is good news, as most of the time you do not want to replace a response pattern with an opposite one. Instead, you usually just need to soften the response, so it no longer generates inappropriate emotions and self-defeating behaviors. Looking at our example of perfectionism, while it is inappropriate to become overly upset and dwell on small mistakes like Sharon, it would be appropriate to be disappointed for a moment, and then move on to other things.

Something that Sharon found to be very useful in reducing her perfectionism was the creation of a summary sheet.

SUMMARY SHEETS

Chapter 5 described how core response patterns that cause inappropriate emotions and problem behaviors usually have four parts:

- Beliefs
- Habitual thinking patterns that distort reality
- Habitual behaviors
- Unconscious conditioned emotional responses

Summary sheets allow you to address each of these four areas in a systematic manner. To create a summary sheet, begin by listing the simple description that describes the response at the top of the page. Next, create four sections that have the following purpose:

Why This Became an Issue

Give a brief description of why the response developed. Often, this includes a simple statement of what might have been true in the past and what is true today. It might also be what lie you believed in the past and what is true today. Use this explanation whenever you catch yourself slipping into circular why questioning because the negative core response has been triggered. It also helps to remind yourself that deeply embedded core responses take time to change.

Situations Where This Causes Problems

Identify specific things you do, think, or say that reflect this core response pattern, along with specific situations where this response is triggered. The more detailed and specific you are, the more the new car principle will help you become aware of times when your response is being triggered.

Things I Can Tell Myself

List specific rational challenges for distorted thinking associated with the response. These are ideas that challenge irrational ideas. When dealing with responses associated with abuse or a difficult childhood environment, include statements that say how the present differs from the past.

Things I Can Do

List specific behaviors you can practice that are the opposite of those associated with the negative response pattern. For example, if you tend to be critical, the opposite would be to practice being encouraging.

Here are the summary sheets that Sharon and Ellie created.

Mistakes Are Terrible/I Need to Do Things Perfectly

Why This Became an Issue.

My mother was a highly respected teacher at the college where she worked and had high expectations for me. While she tried to be positive and encourage me, I was always very aware of when I had fallen short of her expectations. I also copied many of her behaviors when she made a mistake. She would exaggerate the importance of it and make lots of should/must statements. Both of my parents love me and are proud of me. While it's good to enjoy doing things well, I no longer have to be like my mother and expect perfection.

Situations Where This Causes Problems

- At home, work, and in social situations, I often focus on things that don't meet my perfectionistic standards.

- In situations where I've made a mistake of some kind, I become angry and will often dwell on how awful it was.

- I am often critical of how my children do homework and chores.

- I constantly point out my husband's mistakes.

Things I Can Tell Myself

- Mistakes are unavoidable. They are a natural part of the learning process.

- Most mistakes are unimportant in the long run. Ask myself, "Is this error going to be a major life-changing event? Will it be important a week or a month from now?"

- While I like to do things well, most things in life do not require perfection.

- Perfection is impossible to achieve. Humans never do anything perfectly. There's always room for improvement.

- If my goal is perfection, I've guaranteed failure.

- Remember that perfection is a direction, not a place.

- Be pleased when I do things well.

- Let my children be children. Don't expect them to do things like an adult.

- Remind myself that change takes time.

Things I Can Do

- When I catch myself nitpicking at something, stop and find something positive to comment on.

- Practice giving compliments and building others up. Become an encourager, rather than a discourager.

- When doing less important tasks, allow a small flaw or mistake to go uncorrected.
- Notice specific things my kids do that are positive and say something encouraging.
- Say, "Thank you," when people do things, even if they don't meet my expectations.
- Be kind and accepting when I see others make mistakes. This is especially important for my family.
- When I make a mistake, change my focus from how awful it is to finding a solution by asking:
  - o What exactly happened?
  - o Can it be corrected? If so, how? If not, move on.
  - o What have I learned from this mistake? Is there any way I could avoid making the same mistake in the future? (Remember that there are some things that you can't prepare for or prevent.)

As Ellie thought about her behavior, she realized that she often felt that she was not as competent as others. This often prevented her from saying what she thought if it differed from what someone else was saying. It also caused her to be overly cautious and avoid trying new things. Here is the summary sheet she created for this core response pattern:

I'm Not as Smart or Capable as Others
Why This Became an Issue
My brothers teased me a lot when I was young. They constantly called me stupid and laughed at my ideas. Because I

was the youngest, I didn't realize that they knew more than me because they were older. I just thought it was because I was stupid. I was on my own a lot. Because I was a child, I didn't realize that many of the things I struggled with were simply because I received little help from my parents. This was especially true with school. I rarely received any help when I was struggling. This was especially true with math. It seemed so easy for so many other kids. I now realize that they were being helped at home.

Situations Where This Creates Problems

- Whenever I make a mistake, I call myself "stupid" and ridicule myself.
- I worry a lot about people noticing my mistakes and thinking I'm incompetent. Even when I'm doing things that I'm good at, I act as if I'll be found out and people will see I'm really not as good as most.
- I tend to "freeze" whenever I'm asked to give an opinion or when I need to make a decision.
- I apologize a lot when I give an opinion, and I belittle my own ideas.
- I avoid trying new things that I'm unfamiliar with.

Things I Can Tell Myself

- I may not be a genius, but I'm not stupid either. I'm normal, and that is all I need to be. I have many strong qualities and abilities: I'm a great waitress; regulars ask for me when they come to the restaurant. People like to talk to me. I care about others. I am able to help others with their problems. I often see possibilities that others can't see. My manager and coworkers see me as quite clever.

- You don't have to be a genius to be happy and successful. I'm as smart and capable as most others. That is good enough.

- Tell myself that it's OK to slip into old patterns from time to time. Old habits never completely go away.

Things I Can Do

- Whenever I notice that I'm putting myself down or using negative labels, stop and use an opposite positive label.

- Stop comparing myself to others. When I catch myself doing this, remind myself that there will always be people more skilled as well as less skilled at whatever I am doing. It doesn't matter because I'm not in a race with anyone. No one is keeping a score on how I do.

- When someone gives me a compliment, just say, "Thank you."

- Do not apologize when I give an opinion. Simply state it. Do not add things like "This probably isn't very good. . ."

- When asked for my opinion, if I get anxious, say, "Let me think about this for a moment." Slowing things down removes the time pressure I feel and helps me think more clearly.

- Tell myself, "Good job" when I use my new behaviors.

- As you look at summary sheets like the above two, keep in mind that people dealing with the same issues might construct their summary sheets differently. For a summary sheet to be effective, it needs to use ideas and activities that are specific to your experiences, beliefs, and way of thinking.

• The next chapter will explore emotions that seem to come out of the blue.

SUMMARY OF KEY POINTS

• Simple phrases or sentences are often used to describe patterns of behavior and emotional responses that developed in childhood.

• Using labels to identify patterns of distorted thinking and associated conditioned emotional responses helps you become fully conscious of them.

• Labels for a response pattern are based on the idea: "If you act as if you have a particular core response pattern, speak as if you have a particular core response pattern, and think as if you have a particular core response pattern, this pattern is part of who you are."

• Everyone has a combination of positive and negative core response patterns.

• Negative core response patterns may only be triggered in limited settings, such as with family, friends, or at work.

• All traits exist on a continuum. For example, extreme perfectionism is at one end of a continuum with no concern for mistakes or how well or poorly a task is done at the other.

• Often, a negative response pattern is just an exaggeration of what is generally a positive pattern.

- When working to reduce inappropriate emotions and self-defeating behaviors associated with a negative core response pattern, it's usually only necessary to soften it, so it approaches the middle of the continuum.

- Summary sheets allow you to address the different areas of a negative response pattern in a systematic manner. They usually contain four sections:

  o Why this became an issue
  o Situations where this causes problems
  o Things I can tell myself
  o Things I can do

THINGS TO DO

- Look at the list of positive and negative response patterns and identify those that describe how you react in various situations.

- Identify at least one response pattern that you have, either positive or negative, that is not listed and create a label for it.

- Use the ideas in this chapter to create a four-part summary sheet for a negative response pattern that you would like to change. Follow the guidelines given in the chapter. If you're having difficulty with any of the four areas, ask a trusted friend who knows you well for help.

Chapter 8:

Forbidden Emotions

But be sure that human feelings can never be completely stilled.
If they are forbidden from their normal course, like a river, they
will cut another channel through the life and flow out to curse
and ruin and destroy.

– A.W. Tozer

This chapter looks at emotions that are suppressed whenever they are experienced because they have become unacceptable. Unfortunately, emotions like these can never be completely buried. They sneak out from time to time and cause a person to do things that leave them wondering, "Why did I do that?"

WHY DO SOME EMOTIONS BECOME UNACCEPTABLE?

When you look at a young child, you see sa storm of emotions. Indeed, one of the primary developmental tasks for children is learning to manage emotions in a way that enables them to become happy and successful adults who can:

- Accept all of their emotions as normal
- Clearly identify the emotion experienced
- Clearly identify what is generating the emotion
- Use socially appropriate coping skills for managing intense emotions
- Choose effective and socially appropriate behaviors to address the need, threat, or loss triggering the emotion

Unfortunately, during this process, children often learn that some emotions should not be experienced. These emotions then get pushed out of conscious awareness whenever they're experienced.

Emotions that most frequently come to be seen as unacceptable fall into two main categories. The first are emotions associated with weakness. This is usually the result of children learning that they always need to be strong. When they become adults, they will suppress the disappointment or sadness associated with defeat to appear strong. Sometimes the tender feelings associated with intimacy can also be felt as weakness.

Jeremy grew up in a family with a father who had a core response pattern of "always be strong and never show weakness." One way that his father passed this core response along to his son was through direct instruction. Jeremy remembered a time when he was learning to ride a bike. When he fell and scraped his knee, he ran over to his dad, crying. His father responded by saying, "Stop crying. Boys don't cry. Now, be a man; get up and let's try again."

Jeremy's father also displayed the need to always be strong by minimizing any pain or distress he might have in the face of an injury or loss. When asked how he was feeling, he would say, "It's no big deal. Things happen. You get over it and move on." He would then change the subject.

The need to be strong not only caused Jeremy to suppress physical and emotional pain, but it also interfered with his ability to experience the sense of vulnerability associated with intimacy. To Jeremy, this felt like weakness. For example, while watching a tender moment in a movie, he would either find some way to make a joke about it or find something he needed to do.

The second type of emotion that children can learn to avoid is anger. Sometimes this is because of growing up in a culture that has strong prohibitions against expressing anger. It can also result from an environment where confrontation with adult caregivers results in physical or emotional harm. When this is the case, any anger that might prompt the child to confront caregivers is suppressed. Let's look at this response in Julia.

Julia's parents were overly strict with her. If she confronted them in any way, they would respond with intense anger and belittling remarks. Because she was a sensitive child, this was very scary. Even when she did things typical of children, such as spilling something or making a mistake, they would say things like, "Look what you've done! How could you be so stupid?" or "How many times do I have to tell you. . .?" Julia learned to avoid the wrath of her parents by suppressing her anger and avoiding any conflict with them. The core response pattern that developed was "anger and conflict are dangerous."

As an adult, Julia never displayed anger and would only rarely do anything that might cause conflict with others. For example, during a friendly lunch, one of Julia's single friends made an unkind remark about how Julia was not raising her children correctly. Even though this was not true, Julia said nothing. She just smiled and nodded in agreement, then changed the subject.

A more extreme example can be seen in Max, who grew up in a country ruled by a harsh dictatorship. People who spoke up against the government were severely punished. To survive, Max learned to always be calm and quiet when in public. He learned this lesson both by being told to always comply with whatever was asked and by watching what happened to others who challenged government or military officials.

Eventually, Max moved to a country where people had the freedom to do what they want and question the government. However, the core response pattern of "conflict is dangerous" caused him to continue avoiding any sort of confrontation and suppress angry feelings he might have.

SECONDARY EMOTIONS

Emotions that need to be suppressed because they have become unacceptable are often covered by a different, more acceptable emotion. When this is done, the emotion that allows people to hide from an unacceptable emotion is called a secondary emotion. Jeremy not only avoided tender feelings that a movie might trigger, but he would also become angry whenever weak emotions such as shame, guilt, embarrassment, and fear were felt.

While anger was usually an inappropriate response to these situations, it triggered a fight-or-flight response that would flood his body with adrenaline and produce a physical sensation of strength.

Feeling physically strong covered the sense of emotional weakness or vulnerability.

By the time a person is an adult, the use of a secondary emotion to avoid an unacceptable one usually becomes a well-practiced and mostly unconscious habit. Often, it generates a robotic and inappropriate response. This happens because the suppression of an unacceptable emotion with a secondary emotion takes tremendous mental energy. This leaves little left for dealing with current circumstances. Jeremy's quick and almost automatic response when someone asked about how he was doing when injured or having suffered a loss is a good example of this.

The robotic and often inappropriate response that occurs when someone is using their mental resources to suppress an emotion provides a way to identify them. Whenever you identify a recurring emotional response that seems inappropriate, it may indicate you are using a secondary emotion to avoid an unacceptable emotion.

A good example of this is the way I reacted to embarrassment in my younger years. Soon after getting married, my wife and I moved to Japan, where I taught science and math at an international school for two years. As we were settling in, we would periodically go to a local department store. After being at the store for a short time, I would become irritable and start making critical remarks about whatever my wife was doing. After several trips, she pointed this out to me.

Upon reflection, I realized I was embarrassed because I knew very little Japanese and often was uncertain of how to respond in a culturally appropriate way. In my family, avoiding mistakes and being right were important. Embarrassment was not acceptable because it felt like weakness and indicated that I had made some type of blunder. So, I covered up my embarrassment with anger and distracted myself by criticizing my wife. After I identified what was going on, I used the "what's happening, what's real" approach described in Chapter 3 to become comfortable with embarrassment. Whenever I noticed myself becoming uncomfortable in a department store with my wife, I would mentally say:

> "I'm embarrassed because I can't communicate the way I want to and I don't know how to act correctly. I get angry because in my family we always needed to be strong and in control. It's okay to be embarrassed and make mistakes. While I don't like it, it won't kill me. I don't need to run away from it by attacking my wife."

When I challenged my anger with a statement like this, it would immediately disappear and be replaced with embarrassment. At first, my embarrassment would last for several minutes. However, after a short time, I found I would experience a flash of embarrassment that would quickly pass as I acknowledged I felt like a fish out of water. By the end of my time in Japan, it was easy for me to say that I was feeling a little embarrassed when I wasn't sure how to act. I still don't like the feeling of embarrassment. I just don't have to run from it any longer.

As you identify situations where you use a secondary emotion to cover an unacceptable one, develop a brief statement you can say to yourself to become aware of the underlying emotion. If you are thinking about a situation like this later, mentally go back to the situation where you avoided the emotion and allow yourself to experience it. Then, create a "what's happening, what's real" statement. Rehearse the statement a few times and then recall the situation and emotion again. Note how this decreases the intensity of what you're feeling.

As you identify the situations that trigger unacceptable emotions, it becomes easier to identify what is happening in the middle of the experience. At these times:

- Identify the emotion you are experiencing
- Identify the reason you are experiencing the emotion
- Remind yourself that this emotion is normal and safe
- Remind yourself that you can manage your emotions and choose appropriate actions
- Identify what you believe would be an appropriate response

If you're not able to do this because you are in the middle of something that needs your attention or the unacceptable emotion feels too intense, take time later to do the above. Working through unacceptable emotions at a later time reduces their intensity and enables you to accept and manage them more effectively when you experience them.

EMOTIONS CONNECTED TO CHILDHOOD PAIN

Emotions that are unacceptable are usually connected to negative core response patterns that developed when you were young. Because of this, experiencing unacceptable emotions may cause you to recall painful childhood events that were forgotten. This gives you the opportunity to look at these childhood events as an adult and reinterpret both the experiences and the emotions that were too difficult to deal with as a child.[15]

---

[15] Reinterpreting emotions associated with painful experiences is often referred to as "emotional processing."

Sometimes, the emotions connected to painful childhood memories can feel overwhelming. However, as you take time to reinterpret painful past events from an adult perspective, the intensity of the emotions lessens. As you quiet the triggers associated with painful childhood memories, the emotions connected to them will only be triggered in situations where they are an appropriate response. During these times you will experience them without the need to suppress them. You will also find yourself able to choose more effective actions.

Reinterpreting emotions associated with painful childhood experiences involves the following steps:

Find a Safe and Quiet Place to Explore the Past

When working on your own, it's important to find a safe and quiet place where you will not be disturbed.

Give Yourself Time to Explore Painful Memories That Surface

When dealing with painful memories from childhood, you need to give yourself time so you can work through them fully. If you experience memories or emotions from the past when you are in a situation, where you cannot explore the memory that surfaced, such as at work, remind yourself:

"This is just something from the past. I am an adult now. It cannot harm me or control me. I will deal with it later. Right now, I need to focus on the task at hand."

After thinking or saying this, find something to do that will distract you from the memory and the emotions associated with it. Be sure to then revisit this memory later when you have time to work through it. Do not continue to ignore and suppress a memory that continues to resurface. If it's surfacing, it's time to deal with it. If you don't, it will continue to resurface and cause problems, usually at inconvenient times. It is wiser to deal with it at a time and place of your choosing.

Remind Yourself of These Truths About Painful Childhood Events

- This event was in the past. It is no longer part of the present.
- The emotions at that time were appropriate for the situation.
- If the situation resulted from emotional, physical, or sexual abuse, it was not my fault. The perpetrator is the sole person responsible for my mistreatment.
- Today is different.
  o As an adult, I can manage emotions that were overwhelming for me as a child.
  o As an adult, I can do many things that a child cannot do. Be specific, for example: "I can get help and protect myself in ways that a child cannot," "I am stronger," "I can speak up," or "I can leave."
  o These circumstances will never happen again. Be specific as to why this is true. For example, maybe the people involved in the experience are dead or no longer part of your life.

Reinterpret the Memory from an Adult Perspective

The beliefs and thoughts associated with painful childhood memories were those of a child. Ask yourself, "What would I think if I saw a child experiencing this?" Then remind yourself of this answer as you again consider the events that you remembered. If you are dealing with very painful memories, it's often helpful to write a statement about the events you recalled. Here is an example of a statement Julia wrote in response to memories she had of being terrified of her parents' anger when she did things that all children do:

"I was a sensitive child with parents who were overly strict and disciplined me in ways that were too severe. I learned to swallow any anger and avoid conflict. Now I am an adult. I realize I am not bad or less than others. I have the right to speak up when mistreated or when I need something. When I suffer injustice, it's okay to be angry. I'm able to manage my anger and use it to correct injustice in an appropriate manner."

You Don't Need to Do This on Your Own

If at any time you encounter emotions or memories that seem overwhelming, seek help. There are many types of support groups and therapists who can help people heal from childhood wounds. Guidelines for selecting a therapist and finding self-help groups are in Appendixes 1 and 2 at the back of this book.

What If I Frequently Have Emotions That Generate the Urge to Harm Myself or Others?

If you experience frequent emotions that are urging you to harm yourself or others, it's vital to seek help. A professional therapist can help you identify the reason you're experiencing them. A good therapist can then help you work through whatever the source is and provide you with skills for managing hurts from the past and present needs, so they no longer generate these types of emotions. Appendix 1 at the back of this book offers guidelines for finding a therapist.

You will probably have to go through these steps multiple times as wounds from the past, along with the automatic responses they trigger, take time to heal. This is especially true if you've been avoiding them for years. Most find that the intensity of the emotions associated with painful memories lessens as they repeat the above steps. So, even though reconnecting with emotions that you've avoided takes time, the effort is well worth it. Healing from past wounds helps you manage your emotions more effectively and choose behaviors that both enhance your relationships and make you more effective in life.

The next chapter explores emotional responses connected to defense mechanisms, along with ways to reconnect with emotions that you may have avoided in the past.

SUMMARY OF KEY POINTS

- One of the primary developmental tasks of childhood is learning to manage emotions.

- Sometimes people learn that an emotion should not be experienced.

- The emotions that most frequently come to be seen as unacceptable are emotions associated with weakness and anger.

- Children learn that an emotion should be suppressed because: they were taught to suppress it, they copied the behavior of the adults around them who were suppressing an emotion, or because suppressing an emotion protected them.

- A secondary emotion can be used to cover an unacceptable emotion. By the time a person is an adult, the use of a secondary emotion to avoid an unacceptable one is usually a well-practiced and partly unconscious habit accompanied by robotic and inappropriate behavior.

- Unacceptable emotions are usually connected to a negative core response pattern that developed when a person was young. Identifying the events that caused an emotion to become unacceptable provides an opportunity to look at those events as an adult and reinterpret both the experiences and the emotions that were too difficult to deal with as a child.

- When an inappropriate behavior and secondary emotion are identified, use the "what's happening, what's real" approach described in Chapter 3 to become fully aware of the underlying emotion.

- While it may be uncomfortable, you will deal with the situation that triggered the response more appropriately.

- Emotions associated with childhood wounds often need to be reinterpreted from an adult perspective so they can be experienced more appropriately.

- With time and practice, emotions that were dangerous or unacceptable can be experienced appropriately.

- If you encounter emotions or memories that seem overwhelming, seek help. There are many types of support groups and therapists who can help people heal from childhood wounds.

THINGS TO DO

- The things that shaped how you experience emotions while growing up are usually a mixed bag of both positive and negative experiences. The result is that while you may have difficulty with some emotions, you probably manage most of your emotions well. In this exercise, it is equally important to identify the strengths in your past and present, as well as the weaknesses.

  Identify specific forces in your past that helped shape your emotional responses.

  o How did the people who raised me manage anger, fear, disappointment, sadness, and hurt?

  o How did they express joy, excitement, hope, tenderness, and love?

  o What am I doing now that is like what they did?

  o How did the way I managed emotions when young benefit me?

  o How did my place in the family (status, birth order, role, etc.) shape the way I managed my emotions?

  o How did the way I managed my emotions either protect me or provide me with some benefit?

- Examine the past few months and see if there were any times when you were covering an unacceptable emotion with a secondary emotion. These are often times when you experienced anger or anxiety and did something inappropriate. Explore the following for any you identify:

o What was going on just before I reacted?

o Was there a different emotion, if even for a moment, before I felt angry or anxious? While there may be more than one, the one closest to when you felt angry or anxious is usually the one that is being avoided.

o Another way to identify emotions that might be hiding under a secondary one is to look at the situation as if you're looking at a scene in a movie and ask yourself:

o What would this character be feeling?

o How would they react?

You can also ask yourself:

o How would someone I know who handles their emotions well react in this type of situation?

• If disturbing memories surface while you're doing any of these exercises, use the suggestions in this chapter to manage the emotions that the memories awaken. If the work associated with these exercises seems overwhelming, STOP AND SEEK HELP FROM A PROFESSIONAL. Guidelines for selecting a therapist are offered in Appendix 1 at the back of this book.

• As you continue to work on a negative core response pattern you wish to soften, it helps to periodically revise the summary sheet you created with new ideas or insights you have gained. Here are summary sheets that Jeremy and Julia created. They may suggest additional ideas for a summary sheet you are creating.

Always Be Strong and Never Show Weakness
Why This Became an Issue
This is a core response pattern that my dad had. I just copied his example. He also taught me this by telling me that men don't cry and minimizing times when I was hurt or afraid.

Situations Where This Creates Problems
- During times when people are hurt or grieving, I feel the need to cheer them up.
- When I make a mistake or do something foolish, I become angry and blame others.
- Whenever something touches me deeply, such as a sad scene in a movie, I immediately need to hide my soft feelings by making a joke or changing the subject.
- When my children are sad, I try to make them feel better rather than encouraging them to explain what's bothering them.
- When my children are hurt, I immediately tell them to be strong and ignore it.

Things I Can Tell Myself
- Being strong and able to ignore pain has helped me in many situations. However, running away from situations where I'm feeling vulnerable or weak has caused a distance between me and those I care about.

- True intimacy requires me to show and share my soft side with people I'm close to.
- It's okay to admit that I made a mistake or did something stupid. People who matter accept me as I am.
- There is nothing weak or demeaning about choosing to express normal, healthy emotions in appropriate ways to people I love and who love me. It's actually a sign of self-acceptance and trust and an important part of true intimacy. It's also necessary for my mental health.
- When someone I love hurts, it's healthy and loving to listen without trying to fix them. I do not need to "make them strong."

Things I Can Do

- Whenever I notice a mistake or do something stupid, I can admit it and allow myself to feel embarrassed. It will get easier with time.
- When my children have a problem or get hurt, I can acknowledge their feelings and listen to them. Often, this is all that is needed.
- When something like a movie or a song causes me to become emotional, I can allow myself to experience it without saying anything. If I shed a tear or look sad, I don't need to cover it up.

Anger and Conflict Are Dangerous

Why This Became an Issue

As a child, I was afraid to do anything that might make my parents angry. I learned to be passive and avoid conflict. This became a habit that I took into school and then into my adult life.

Situations Where This Creates Problems

- When someone says something that I don't think is true, I nod in agreement rather than say I disagree.
- I allow others to make choices for me, such as at a restaurant or while watching television.
- I am passive at work and rarely give my opinion.
- When I see something that is not correct, I remain silent.
- Sometimes, I find it hard to correct my children's misbehavior.

Things I Can Tell Myself

- My parents were wrong about how they disciplined me. It made me swallow my anger whenever it was felt.
- It's normal to become angry when something is causing problems. I can feel angry and choose appropriate ways to speak up.
- It's important to correct my children's misbehavior. They need to learn how to behave in order to be successful adults.
- Reasonable and mature people can handle being told what I honestly believe. They won't think less of me or attack me.
- Conflict is a normal part of life. I can resolve normal conflicts in a friendly way with my partner and reasonable adults.

Things I Can Do

- I can express my honest opinion with others. I can start with times when we're talking about less important things, like current events or movies.

- I can say I don't like something.
- I can make my own decisions when I'm with others. I don't need to always do what they want.
- I can tell my partner when I don't like a particular movie or program and say that I want to watch something else.

Chapter 9:

Making Friends
with Your Emotions

*If we ignore and repress an emotion, we won't erase its message
— we'll just shoot the messenger and interfere with
an important natural process.*

– Karla McLaren

In previous chapters, you explored conditioned emotional responses that cause inappropriate emotions that seem to come out of nowhere and generate inappropriate actions. You also looked at the various ways people hide from unpleasant emotions. This chapter discusses how to hear more clearly the messages that your emotions are giving you so you can make better decisions about the actions, if any, to take.

COGNITIVE DISSONANCE

Leon Festinger introduced the world to the term "cognitive dissonance" in 1957 to describe the discomfort you feel when there is a conflict between your beliefs and some aspect of reality. One type of cognitive dissonance occurs when facts that people believe are true conflict with their behavior. For example, Logan knows that being active is important for his health, but he works at a job that requires him to sit most of the day. Dr. Sanders continues to smoke, even though he is fully aware it is bad for his health.

Cognitive dissonance also occurs when facts or some aspect of reality conflict with a strongly held belief. For example, Emma refuses to believe a news account that describes misconduct by someone she holds in high esteem. Reese just read about a scientific study that conflicts with his belief that a glass of wine each day is good for his health.

The cognitive dissonance that occurs with conflicts like this can generate negative emotions, such as:

- Anxiety
- Anger
- Sadness
- Regret
- Shame

Emotions like these can be beneficial when they prompt a person to resolve a conflict by making a positive change in behavior. Dr. Sanders decides that it's time to quit smoking. Logan starts going to a gym after work.

The negative emotions generated by cognitive dissonance can also prompt people to reexamine what they believe about themselves, others, or the world. Emma looks for other information that would confirm or refute what was reported. Reese looks at additional information on the pros and cons of having a glass of wine each day.

When you respond to cognitive dissonance by taking an honest look at why you are doing something or holding certain beliefs, it helps you become more effective in life. However, people who are afraid of or don't want to change and those with very rigid beliefs will use one or more of the following defense mechanisms to avoid any discomfort that might come from cognitive dissonance.

COMMON DEFENSE MECHANISMS

The idea of psychological defense mechanisms was first proposed by Sigmund Freud in 1894. However, theories about defense mechanisms have evolved over time. Today, they are seen as mostly unconscious responses that protect people from experiencing negative emotions generated by unwanted thoughts, impulses, memories, and aspects of reality that conflict with their behavior or beliefs about themselves, others, or the world. Dozens of different defense mechanisms have been identified. However, we'll just look at how six are used to quiet the negative emotions produced by cognitive dissonance.

While defense mechanisms are often thought of as something negative, they are a normal and often healthy part of life. They can help people navigate painful experiences and channel their energy more productively. Defense mechanisms only become problematic when used too frequently or if they are used too long and the emotions and conflicts they are protecting you from are never addressed positively.

The way we use defense mechanisms is intimately connected with our core response patterns. As explained in Chapter 7, core response patterns result from several factors:

- Our inborn predispositions
- Emotions connected to positive, and negative experiences we had in childhood
- Responses that were taught to us directly or adopted by modeling after the adults who raised us
- Habitual ways of thinking
- Conscious beliefs we come to hold about ourselves, others, and the world

The following six defense mechanisms are used regularly in everyday life to avoid the negative feelings that cognitive dissonance produces.

Repression

Repression is the unconscious blocking of unpleasant emotions, impulses, memories, and thoughts from your conscious mind. You have no awareness of the unacceptable emotion or the thing triggering it. A person who is repressing memories, thoughts, or emotions might have difficulty talking about their thoughts or feelings and may even become defensive when asked about them.

Chapter 8 described how Max's passivity helped him survive in a country ruled by a harsh dictatorship. His passivity was only possible because much of the anger he felt because of the injustice all around him was pushed completely out of conscious awareness. Max found the ideas in the last chapter helped him become aware of times when anger was signaling that an important need was not being met. This allowed him to notice things that he needed to address, such as his reluctance to ask for a pay raise. Becoming more in touch with his anger also gave him the motivation to act.

Suppression

Suppression is like repression, but with suppression, you consciously choose to block awareness of the unacceptable emotion, impulse, memory, or thought. The most common way we do this is to focus on an activity unrelated to the source of the negative emotions. It allows both the surgeon in the middle of a complex surgery and the grade-school teacher with a classroom full of children to focus on the immediate task at hand while negative emotions connected to problems in other areas of their lives are moved out of conscious awareness. This use of suppression is appropriate if you take time later to deal with the issues generating the negative emotions you've suppressed in a direct and healthy manner.

Sandy was at a family gathering when she became irritated with her husband's behavior. Because of the people around her, she thought, "I can forget about this for now and talk to him later." This allowed her to suppress her anger and focus her attention on her family. Later, she talked to her husband about what caused her reaction.

The overuse of suppression becomes a problem when it blocks your awareness of the need to address important issues. People who want to avoid negative feelings produced by cognitive dissonance will often distract themselves with an activity, or choose to think about something unrelated to the distressing thoughts and feelings. An example would be the way Jeremy, who you met in Chapter 8, would suppress tender feelings he associated with weakness by telling a joke, or becoming busy with something unrelated to whatever was triggering his unwanted emotions. Another all too common and destructive way to suppress unwanted thoughts and feelings is to numb oneself with alcohol or drugs.

For some, the continued suppression of negative emotions triggered by cognitive dissonance can trigger a stress reaction in the body. This can cause things such as skin conditions, high blood pressure, and back, neck, chest, or abdominal pain.

Denial

Denial is probably one of the best-known defense mechanisms. It refers to situations where you refuse to face reality or admit to an obvious truth. External events or circumstances are blocked from your mind, so you don't have to deal with their emotional impact.

This isn't always a bad thing. When dealing with something shocking or distressing, such as the death of a loved one or receiving a serious diagnosis, being in denial can give you a little time and space to gradually, often unconsciously, come to grips with the situation. Common forms of denial include:

- You refuse to talk about the problem.
- You find ways to justify your behavior.
- You blame other people or outside forces for causing the problem.
- You persist in a behavior despite negative consequences.
- You promise to address the problem in the future.
- You avoid thinking about the problem.

People in denial of an important problem sometimes feel hopeless or helpless because, on some level, they know the problem is being ignored. It's also common to brush off the concerns of others when they offer advice or help. Someone like this might pretend to agree or tell others to mind their own business. Sometimes people in denial avoid people or situations that make the conflict obvious. For example, Mason, who is 75, avoids making a will or going to the funerals of friends because of his fear of death.

Chapter 8 introduced Jeremy, who would say that everything is fine whenever he was hurt or suffered a loss. After reading about this defense mechanism, Jeremy added the following to his summary sheet in the "Things I Can Do" section:

- When I am in pain or disappointed, I can admit it to those who care about me, especially my wife.

Over time, Jeremy was pleased to see that telling his wife when he was disappointed made him feel even closer to her.

Rationalization

Rationalization is the use of false but seemingly rational or logical reasons to explain failures, mistakes, weaknesses, or contradictions that we do not want to accept or deal with. We use rationalizations when we're confronted with things we've done or facts that conflict with our beliefs about ourselves, others, or the world.

In areas of your life where you hold rigid beliefs, you probably use rationalizations to resolve conflicts so well that you don't experience any negative emotions. At other times, they are a way to calm the emotions that a conflict causes.

Sharon, who you met in Chapter 7, used rationalizations to explain how any mistake she made resulted from something other than herself. Her use of rationalizations allowed her to maintain the illusion that she never made mistakes. This need was driven by the discomfort she felt when reality conflicted with her core response pattern of "mistakes are terrible/I need to do things perfectly." After reading about rationalization she added the following to her summary sheet in the "Things I Can Do" section:

- When I make a mistake, I can admit it rather than looking for someone or something to blame for it.

With time, she became comfortable with saying that she made a mistake or did something wrong. This helped her become less critical of others. It also helped her to more easily focus on what could be done to correct the mistake instead of looking for something to blame for it.

Intellectualization

Intellectualization is the use of reasoning to avoid experiencing uncomfortable emotions. By channeling mental energy into a logical assessment or abstract discussion, an individual can avoid painful emotions or remain distanced from beliefs that challenge their sense of self.

This is what Jeremy did when his mother died. He avoided the grief and sadness he felt by focusing all his energy on funeral arrangements and taking care of others. Later, he was puzzled by his lack of interest in things he normally enjoyed and by how he became irritated at little things such as slow traffic or spilling his coffee.

After reading about intellectualization, he took some time alone with his wife to tell her about how much he missed his mother. He could also tell her in the days afterwards when he was feeling sad. He was surprised to find that the irritation he felt over small things went away. Instead, as was discussed in Chapter 8, the secondary emotion of anger was replaced with what he was really feeling–the sadness over his loss. While this was uncomfortable, it allowed Jeremy to treat others more kindly. Giving himself time to mourn his mother also allowed his grief to diminish and his interest in normal activities to return.

Displacement

Displacement is the redirection of negative emotions away from their original source to a less threatening one. Like many defense mechanisms, displacement can occur subconsciously. While you often need to suppress negative emotions in one setting, taking time to consciously deal with them later keeps you from unconsciously displacing them onto others. A positive example would be telling a friend or partner about a frustrating day.

Because Jeremy's core response pattern of "always be strong and in control" did not allow him to deal with weakness consciously, he processed it unconsciously. After losing an important sale because of a mistake that his manager had made, he was angry. However, instead of talking to his manager, he became angry at a clerk in a store he stopped by after work. When he arrived home, he said hurtful things to his wife.

Realizing that he often displaced negative emotions he had at work onto others, especially his wife, Jeremy also added the following to the "Things I Can Do" section of his summary sheet:

- When I've had a bad day, take some time after work to think about it. This allows me time to cool down and decide what, if anything, I might need to do about it. I can also tell my wife that I had a bad day, so she understands why I might be in a bad mood. Then, I can ask her to give me some time to think things through.

Listening to the Messages Your Emotions Bring

In Chapter 8, you learned how the deeper, unconscious part of your mind is constantly making associations between the events you experience and the things you have identified as satisfying a need or representing a threat or loss. You also learned how this part of your mind is constantly using these associations to evaluate the events taking place around you. Whenever a connection is made, it generates an emotion. The job of the conscious, thinking part of the brain is to listen to these messages and decide what, if any, action should be taken. When you ignore these messages, you are ignoring things that are important and which can interfere with your ability to lead a happy and successful life.

Previous chapters have also detailed how an event will sometimes generate an inappropriate emotion that is too intense or that is an illogical response to the situation you are in because of associations with painful events in the past, distorted thinking, and irrational beliefs. Even when this happens, the message is still important to hear. It gives you the opportunity to use the tools you've been learning to reinterpret the past from an adult perspective, practice new ways of thinking, and replace old, self-defeating behaviors with new, more appropriate ones. Over time, this reduces both the intensity and the number of times that inappropriate emotions are experienced.

One key in being able to clearly hear the messages that your emotions bring is the ability to identify correctly what you are feeling. While this is easy for some, others find it takes time to reconnect with emotions they have been avoiding. However, the benefit is worth the effort. Being able to hear your emotions clearly helps you identify the need, want, threat, or loss that is generating it. This frees up the mental and emotional energy that was used to avoid the unwanted emotion so you can deal with life in a more fully conscious manner. This increases your ability to choose actions that are appropriate and effective.

RECONNECTING WITH UNCOMFORTABLE EMOTIONS

There are two basic steps to reconnect with emotions that have been avoided. First, you identify words you may be using to hide from uncomfortable emotions. Then, you can begin using words that describe what you're feeling more accurately. Here are four common ways that people hide from emotions by shifting their focus away from what they are feeling. Whenever you catch yourself using words like these, take a moment to ask yourself what you are feeling.

Using Words That Describe Your Mental State

People who are uncomfortable with their emotions often use words that describe a mental state in place of words that describe an emotion. This is especially true for people who use intellectualization to hide from unacceptable emotions. For example, a person might say, "I feel confused," when they are afraid, angry, or sad. Confusion is not an emotion. Confusion indicates that you don't understand something. It would be more accurate to say, "I am confused."

Confusion can be a cover for anxiety, anger, or sadness. By focusing on your lack of understanding, you do not have to acknowledge the underlying emotion. Here are several common examples of words that are used in this way:

Baffled	Confounded	Puzzled
Bewildered	Mystified	Stumped
Confused	Perplexed	

Using Words That Describe Circumstances

Another way to hide from emotions is to use words that describe circumstances as if they were emotions. For example, a person might say, "I'm *feeling* frustrated." Frustration describes a circumstance where you are not getting what you want. A person might also say, "I'm *feeling* helpless." This describes a circumstance where you do not have the power or ability to control events and make them turn out the way you want. It would be more accurate to simply say, "I *am* frustrated by this," "I *am* helpless in this situation," or "I *can't do anything* to change things."

A person might also say, "I'm feeling like such a failure." While it may be true that you failed at something, this is an event that then produces an emotion, usually fear, anger, or sadness. In the same way, when frustrated or helpless, the emotion you experience will be anxiety, anger, or sadness. Here are examples of words used in this way:

Beaten	Foiled	Powerless
Defeated	Frustrated	Unfulfilled
Defenseless	Helpless	Vulnerable
Flustered	Impotent	
Failure	Let down	

Using Words That Describe Personal Qualities

A third way to hide from emotions is to substitute words that describe personal qualities for words that describe true emotions or events. For example, a person might say, "I'm *feeling* inadequate." This means that you see yourself as failing to possess some quality or ability that you need to accomplish something. A more accurate statement would be, "I *am* inadequate to deal with this," or "I see myself *as being* inadequate to deal with this." One's perception of being inadequate might then produce anxiety, anger, or sadness.

While the following words are similar to the previous ones, this group of words describes circumstances as more the result of personal deficiencies than those in the previous section.

Hopeless	Pathetic	Weak
Inadequate	Pitiful	Worthless
Inferior	Unfulfilled	
Insignificant	Useless	

Using Words That Are Vague

The fourth way to hide from emotions is to use words that are vague in place of words that identify specific emotions. For example, a person might say, "That's disturbing." How is this disturbing? Is it causing you to be anxious, angry, or sad? Here are examples of words used in this manner:

Bothered	Emotional	Upset
Distressed	Troubled	
Disturbed	Unsettled	

DEVELOPING AN ACCURATE VOCABULARY TO DESCRIBE YOUR EMOTIONS

While there are basically three types of negative emotions—fear, anger, and sadness—the English language has hundreds of words that describe the various levels of intensity for each of them. Chapter 2 used the following diagram to show the full range of these emotions:

Apprehension ———— Fear ————Terror
Irritation ———————Anger ———— Rage
Disappointment ——— Sadness ——— Depression

If using accurate words to describe your emotions is difficult, begin with just the words "happy," "excited," "angry," "afraid," and "sad." Once you feel comfortable with these, expand your emotional vocabulary with words from the following list. Something else that helps people who are usually not aware of their emotions is to identify the things they do when anxious, angry, or sad. Everyone has something they do when they experience these emotions that is unique to them.

Identifying specific behaviors you do when anxious, angry, or sad allows the new car principle discussed in Chapter 5, to alert you to when you are experiencing these emotions. An example of this was presented in Chapter 8, where I described how, while living in Japan, I would react to embarrassment by becoming irritable and critical of my wife.

If it's easy for you to describe the emotions you experience, you may find it helpful to expand your emotional vocabulary so you can be more precise in describing the level of emotion that you are experiencing. The following list offers a good place to start. To keep from being overwhelmed, just select one or two words on the list that you like, but which you do not currently use. Write them on a card. Then, look at the card in the morning to remind yourself to practice using them. Soon, they'll be part of your regular vocabulary. Then select one or two more and practice using them.

Words That Describe Positive Emotions:

Affectionate	Exhilarated	Proud
Amorous	Fond	Relaxed
Amused	Glad	Relieved
Brave	Gratified	Romantic
Calm	Happy	Satisfied
Charmed	Joyful	Sentimental
Cheerful	Jubilant	Serene
Contented	Lighthearted	Surprised
Delighted	Loving	Thrilled
Elated	Overjoyed	Tranquil
Ecstatic	Passionate	Tickled
Euphoric	Peaceful	
Excited	Pleased	

Words That Describe Negative Emotions:

Afraid	Frightened	Jealous
Aggravated	Furious	Melancholy
Angry	Grief-stricken	Mortified

Annoyed	Hateful	Morose
Anxious	Heartbroken	Nervous
Ashamed	Horrified	Outraged
Bored	Humiliated	Repulsed
Burnt out	Hurt	Resentful
Cold	In despair	Sad
Depressed	Incensed	Scared
Disgusted	Infuriated	Terrified
Embarrassed	Intimidated	
Envious	Irritated	

The next two chapters explore what has been discovered by what is sometimes called positive psychology, or "the science of happiness," about the things needed to experience a general sense of contentment and happiness in one's life.

SUMMARY OF KEY POINTS

- Cognitive dissonance describes a condition where there is a conflict between one's beliefs and some aspect of reality.

- Defense mechanisms allow people to quickly resolve conflicts with little emotion. For others, cognitive dissonance can generate negative emotions.

- When negative emotions generate the need to resolve the conflict, they often prompt a positive change in behavior or one's beliefs, so there is no longer a conflict.

- People who don't want to change and those with very rigid beliefs will continue to use one or more defense mechanisms to avoid the discomfort produced by cognitive dissonance.

- Defense mechanisms are automatic unconscious responses that protect people from experiencing negative emotions generated when some aspect of reality conflicts with their behavior or beliefs about themselves, others, or the world.

- Everyone uses defense mechanisms in daily life. They protect us from being overwhelmed by strong emotions when we need to focus on something important that needs our full attention. They only become a problem when overused. Then, they interfere with our ability to deal with life in a fully conscious and effective manner. There are six common defense mechanisms:

  o Denial

  o Repression

  o Suppression

  o Displacement

  o Rationalization

  o Intellectualization

- Emotions are simply information telling you that you need to take action concerning a need, want, threat, or loss. The thinking part of your brain then needs to decide what the best course of action would be.

- Being able to hear your emotions clearly helps you identify the need, want, threat, or loss that is generating it. This frees up the mental and emotional energy that was used to avoid the unwanted emotion so you can deal with life in a more fully conscious manner. This increases your ability to choose actions that are appropriate and effective.

- One way people hide from emotions is to use nonemotional words to describe emotions. There are four ways that people do this:

  o Using words that describe your mental state
  o Using words that describe circumstances
  o Using words that describe personal qualities
  o Using words that are vague

- If identifying emotions accurately is difficult, begin with just the words "happy," "excited," "angry," "afraid," and "sad." Once you feel comfortable with these, add words listed in the chapter to describe the different levels of intensity for each that you experience.

THINGS TO DO

- Add any ideas presented in this chapter that you like to the summary sheets you are working with.

- Identify the defense mechanisms that were used by the people who raised you.

- Identify the defense mechanisms that you frequently use.

- Look at the four ways that words are used to avoid emotions. Make a list of any you use. Then, review the list for a week so the new car principle will help you become aware of when you are using them. Whenever you notice yourself doing this, identify what you are feeling with a word that accurately describes your emotion.

- If you find it difficult to identify the emotions you experience or if you are unaware of what you are feeling, the following activities are useful.

  o Think about times in the past when you have been anxious, afraid, or sad. Identify specific things you did that you do not normally do. You can now use these behaviors to identify times when you are experiencing emotions you are ignoring. Often, just realizing that this behavior is something you do when you're anxious, angry, or sad is enough to allow you to become aware osf what you're feeling.

  o Think about the last day or so. Has anything happened that most would consider a threat or loss? How did you react at that time? How do you feel about the threat or loss now?

    ◆ Take a moment to experience the emotion you are feeling.
    ◆ Then identify the reason you are experiencing this emotion. Be specific.

- Is this a reasonable response? If so, decide what action, if any, you should take to deal with the threat or loss that triggered the emotion.

  o If this is not a reasonable response, what things from your past caused you to react this way?

  o Take time periodically during the day to ask yourself, "What emotion am I feeling right now?" This is even more effective to do after any event that would normally generate intense emotions in the average person.

- If you find it easy to identify what you are feeling, consider whether it would be helpful to expand your emotional vocabulary. If so, look at the list of words for positive and negative emotions. Add a few that you don't normally use to your vocabulary.

- Continue to review your summary sheets at least twice a week.

Chapter 10:

The Science of Happiness

Having someone wonder where you are when you don't come home at night is a very old human need.

– Margaret Mead

This chapter introduces what positive psychology has discovered about the things that promote a general sense of contentment and happiness in one's life. It then explores what has been the most important contributor to a satisfying life: positive relationships.

POSITIVE PSYCHOLOGY: THE SCIENCE OF HAPPINESS

Since the beginnings of psychology in the 1800s, there was little research into well-being, success, and high functioning. That all changed in 1998 with the presidential saddress to the American Psychological Association by University of Pennsylvania psychologist Martin Seligman. In it, he urged psychology to "turn toward understanding and building the human strengths to complement our emphasis on healing damage." The next year, 60 scholars gathered for the first Gallup Positive Psychology Summit; two years later, the conference went international. At the time of this writing, there are hundreds of college courses on positive psychology and a wealth of research being conducted into what leads to a happy life.

While the popular press often refers to positive psychology as the "science of happiness," this is misleading, as happiness can take many different forms and result from a variety of behaviors and life circumstances. Everything from joy and excitement to contentment and love has been associated with happiness. To avoid the confusion that comes with using the word "happiness," researchers use the term "subjective well-being." A basic definition of happiness that positive psychologists use that reflects the ideas of subjective well-being is:

> Happiness is a state characterized by contentment and general satisfaction with one's current situation.

SUBJECTIVE WELL-BEING

Psychologist Ed Diener coined the term subjective well-being in 1984. He identified three different aspects of how people see their own well-being:

- Frequent positive affect: the experience of positive emotions most of the time

- Infrequent negative affect: the experience of negative emotions and moods only occasionally

- Cognitive evaluations: the way people think about their lives and overall life satisfaction

Today, the use of subjective well-being is a common measure of overall life satisfaction, happiness, and well-being in both psychological research and as an indicator of individual health.

How you feel about life is shaped by your personality, habitual ways of thinking, and beliefs as well as by the circumstances and culture in which you live. Because of this, people differ on what brings happiness. A factor that is important to you might be less important to someone else. However, researchers have identified five general areas that play an important role in overall subjective well-being:

Personality and Temperament

While researchers agree that your level of subjective well-being is a combination of genetics and the other factors listed here, they disagree on how large a role genetic factors play. Estimates range from 10% to 50% with a commonly used 40% figure. While this is significant, keep in mind that even if this turns out to be correct, it still leaves 60% of your happiness up to other factors, all of which you have some control over.

Basic Resources

This includes things like money, housing, and health care. While these things are important, research by Daniel Kahneman and Angus Deaton in 2010 found that money only bought happiness up to an income of about $75,000. After that, it had no significant effect on emotional well-being.

Social Factors

This includes factors concerning both the general society in which you live and your specific circumstances, such as crime, war, poverty, and conflict.

Social Support

Social support refers to the various types of support that a healthy network of family, friends, coworkers, and others can provide in times of need. This also includes emotional support that relationships provide in helping you feel valued, accepted, and understood.

Mindset and Resilience

This refers to the habitual ways of thinking and beliefs that shape how you make sense of the world and yourself. Two factors that play an important role are optimism and resilience. Optimism is a mental attitude characterized by hope and confidence in success and a positive future. Resilience is typically defined as the capacity to recover from difficult life events. Many things can cause one to see little chance for success when faced with obstacles and make it difficult to bounce back from setbacks. Two well-researched examples are a low sense of self-efficacy and learned helplessness, as described in Chapters 4 and 5.

The rest of this chapter explores your need for social support, more specifically, the key role that relationships have in allowing you to experience a positive subjective sense of well-being.

THE IMPORTANCE OF POSITIVE RELATIONSHIPS

While many things are identified as contributing a positive sense of well-being, the most important is positive relationships. This is not surprising when looking at the seven emotional circuits described in Chapter 1. Four of them have the specific purpose of helping us form strong relationships. Here is a short recap of these four systems:

CARE – This helps ensure that parents have a strong desire to take care of their offspring. It also plays a role in the formation of friendships and the love you feel towards those you are close to. The CARE and PANIC systems generate feelings of empathy and sympathy when bad things happen to others, but especially to those we love.

PLAY – This system urges young children to engage in physical play like wrestling, running, and chasing each other. This type of play helps them bond socially and learn what behaviors are permissible. Its influence carries over into the many forms of adult play.

PANIC – This produces the distress that babies show when separated from their caregivers. It also generates the sadness you feel when separated from loved ones.

LUST – After this system becomes fully awakened during adolescence, it plays an important role in bonding couples together.

Chapter 2 discussed how these systems along with the other three primary emotional systems–SEEKING/Curiosity (the urge to explore), RAGE/Anger (the urge to protect by attacking), and FEAR/Anxiety (the urge to flee from danger)–all become regulated by the higher thinking part of the brain. It also discussed how the higher cognitive emotions – love, pride, guilt, shame, embarrassment, envy, and jealousy – emerge as associations and beliefs form about oneself, others, and the world. These beliefs and associations shape how people see:

- The roles of men and women
- What is important in life
- What is forbidden
- How success and failure are measured
- How important needs are met

Children who grow up in healthy families develop beliefs, associations, and habitual ways of thinking and acting in each of these five areas that enable them to form healthy, satisfying relationships. Unfortunately, many children grow up in dysfunctional and abusive families. This produces beliefs, associations, and ways of thinking and acting that prevent them from forming satisfying relationships. Often, the void left by the need for a positive relationship is filled with substitutes such as power, fame, success in some area of life, money, drugs, and alcohol.

BENEFITS OF POSITIVE RELATIONSHIPS

The benefits of having positive relationships go beyond just experiencing a higher level of subjective well-being. While many benefits have been reported in connection with having a long-term positive relationship, the following five are most often cited.

Reduced Stress

Having the support of someone who loves you has been shown to help people face life's difficulties, from times of illness to moments of worry and stress. One of the hormones responsible for this is the bonding hormone oxytocin. This is the hormone that gives you the warm and fuzzy feeling you experience when you're cuddling with your significant other. It turns out that it is also a powerful stress reliever. Studies from the University of Chicago and the University of Arizona in Tucson showed that being in the presence of your loved one, or even just thinking about them, boosts oxytocin, which can lower the levels of the two primary stress hormones, adrenaline and cortisol.

Lower Anxiety

Being in a stable, long-term relationship decreases anxiety. One example of this research was conducted by the State University of New York at Stony Brook. The brains of couples in strongly connected relationships were scanned and compared with the brains of people in new relationships. While both groups showed activation in the areas of the brain associated with love, other parts of the brain looked surprisingly different. For the couples in strongly connected relationships, areas associated with bonding were activated but the anxiety-producing areas were less active, unlike the couples in new relationships.

Faster Healing

An example of research in this area was conducted by Ohio State University Medical Center. They found that flesh wounds heal twice as fast when couples regularly had warm interactions with one another, compared to couples who were routinely hostile. The study also revealed that the stress from an ordinary half-hour argument can slow healing by at least one day.

Better Heart Health

Studies have shown that married people face half the risk of dying from heart disease as unmarried or uncoupled people. At the same time, isolation has the exact opposite effect. A 2015 study of national census and death certification data found that over an eight-year period, married people were 14 percent less likely than their unmarried counterparts to die in the hospital after a heart attack. They also stayed in the hospital an average of two days less.

Longer Life

Numerous studies have shown that married persons tend to live longer than their unmarried counterparts. Some reasons that have been given are that married people tend to take fewer risks with their health and have better mental and emotional health. Marriage also provides more social and material support, which means having someone to take you to the doctor or care for you when you are sick. Marriage also offers protection against feelings of loneliness, something that has been documented as a life shortener.

While the above findings were with long-term marriages, they are also probably true of any positive long-term relationship. An indication of this comes from a University of Washington study that found married LGBT study participants reported better physical and mental health, more social support, and greater financial resources than those who were single.

TRAITS OF HEALTHY RELATIONSHIPS

The benefits described above are best gained in healthy long-term relationships. While healthy relationships probably won't have all the traits listed in this section, they will have most of them. That's why it's important to have a network of relationships that might range from romantic to close and casual friends. A trait that is weak in one relationship can be made up for in another. For example, Sharon's husband was a kind and affectionate man who had little interest in her hobbies. Sharon satisfied this need that was not met in her marriage by spending time with a friend who shared her interest in this area.

As you look at the following list, identify relationships where you experience each of them. Make note of any that are lacking in your relationships.

Acceptance

You are accepted as you are. This also means you feel you fit in and belong in their life. This person introduces you to their family and friends and includes you in their activities.

Boundaries

You can have ideas and opinions that are different and take part in activities that do not include this person.

Closeness

You have warm feelings when you are with this person and believe that a strong bond exists between the two of you.

Companionship

You enjoy spending time together.

Concern

This person displays a genuine concern for your welfare, pleasure, and pain.

Constructive Problem-Solving

You can resolve problems, so each person feels good about the solution.

Empathy

This person can see events through your eyes and, to some degree, experience your pain or pleasure, suffering or joy.

Encouragement

You hear frequent encouragement.

Expressions of Affection

You experience frequent affectionate gestures, such as touch, words of affection, or doing something that is important to you.

Independence

You can have ideas and opinions that are different without being criticized or condemned.

Interest

This person takes a genuine interest in the things that are important to you, along with your successes and failures.

Intimacy

This person shares their thoughts and feelings with you, and you feel safe sharing yours with them.

Kindness

This person is considerate and thoughtful in their dealings with you.

Open and Free Communication

You feel free to talk about any subject and explore different ideas.

Priority

This person takes time to be with you.

Safety
You feel physically and emotionally safe.

Sensitivity
This person shows an awareness of and respect for your concerns and vulnerable spots.

Spirituality
This person shares their view of spirituality in a positive way and respects your view.

Support
You have a strong sense that this person is dependable, that you can lean on them during difficult times.

Trust
This person does what they say they will do and does not share those things you want to keep private with others.

Unconditional Love
Love is expressed freely and is not dependent on your good behavior.

More will be said about this exercise in the Things to Do section at the end of this chapter.

SOCIAL MEDIA

The World Happiness Report 2019 reported that by 2018, "95 percent of United States adolescents (13-17) had access to a smartphone, and 45 percent said they were online 'almost constantly.'" These adolescents are now adults who spend hours online. Subsequent studies have found that social media can be a double-edged sword, depending on how it is used.

Professor Derrick Wirtz of the University of British Columbia Okanaga examined the relationship between social media and life satisfaction in a study that focused on how people use three major social platforms: Facebook, Twitter, and Instagram. While face-to-face interactions are associated with satisfaction and contentment, many come away from social media with negative feelings. There are a variety of reasons for this.

Most of what you see on social media is not real. People rarely post negative images of themselves, so you are only getting a carefully selected view where everyone looks happy in photos that are flattering. This one-sided perspective of other people's lives can contribute to negative feelings due to what is called the fear of missing out (FOMO), witnessing people in your network having a good time without you. Spending time passively scrolling on social media can make FOMO cause you to feel like your own life doesn't measure up and that you're missing out on fun things that everyone else is doing.

It's also easy for people who are sad or take part in any form of physical or spiritual self-harm to find groups that validate and amplify such feelings and behavior. For example, there are groups online for people with eating disorders that give tips on how to indulge this illness rather than heal.

Another finding by Wirtz was that people use social media more when they are lonely, but the time spent on social media only increased their feelings of loneliness. One reason is that many casual friends on social media are being used as a substitute for a smaller network of deep, meaningful relationships. In contrast,

German researchers from Ruhr-Universität Bochum found that people who reduced the amount of time they spent on social media by just 20 minutes for two weeks ended up smoking less, being more active, and feeling happier in general. Incredibly, the positive effects of logging off stayed with the participants for months after the experiment concluded.

With all these negatives, there is a positive side to social media. It can help you interact and connect with people who are important to you directly, such as with an online video or chat program. Social media can also provide meaningful contact for people who are housebound to form friendships, get support, receive therapy, and enjoy a better quality of life. Face-to-face interactions with people you love and trust also foster the sharing of bad times and the good times, an important part of true intimacy. This is usually missing in texting and chatting.

This chapter identified positive relationships as being the most important contributor to a sense of subjective well-being. The next chapter explores two additional key elements: purpose and meaning.

SUMMARY OF KEY POINTS

- Positive psychology tries to answer questions about what makes people happy, what a good life is, and how to increase life satisfaction. Positive psychology is sometimes called "the science of happiness."

- Because happiness can take many different forms and result from a variety of behaviors and life circumstances, researchers focus on what is called subjective well-being.

o Frequent positive affect: the experience of positive emotions most of the time

o Infrequent negative affect: the experience of negative emotions and moods only occasionally

o Cognitive evaluations: the way people think about their lives and overall life satisfaction

- Five general areas contribute to one's overall subjective well-being:

o Personality and temperament

o Basic resources

o Social factors

o Mindset and resilience

o Social support

- Of all the things identified as contributing to a positive sense of well-being, the most important is positive relationships. This is not surprising since four of the seven emotional systems help form strong relationships: CARE, PLAY, PANIC, and LUST.

- While a relationship probably won't have all the traits of healthy relationships described in this chapter, healthy relationships have most of them.

- It's important to have a network of relationships so needs that are not met in one relationship are met in another one.

- Many come away from social media with negative feelings because most of what you see on social media is a carefully selected view of people's lives. People rarely choose to post negative and unflattering images.

- The one-sided perspective of other people's lives on social media can contribute to negative feelings because of the fear of missing out (FOMO), witnessing people in your network having a good time without you.

- Spending time passively scrolling on social media can make FOMO cause you to feel like your own life doesn't measure up and that you're missing out on fun things that everyone else is doing.

- Having many casual friends on social media may be used as a substitute for a smaller, personal network of deep, meaningful relationships.

- A positive side to social media is it can help you interact and connect with people who are important to you directly, such as with an online video or chat program.

THINGS TO DO

- Think about how you use social media and check any of the following that apply to you:

  o You are spending more time on social media than with your real-world friends and family members.

  o Your use of your social media is negatively affecting your relationships.

  o You compare yourself unfavorably with others on social media or you find you are frequently jealous of others.

  o You use social media to fight boredom or to deal with loneliness.

o Your work obligations, family life, or schoolwork are suffering because of the time you spend on social media.

o You are being trolled or cyberbullied by others online.

o You are engaging in risky behaviors or taking outrageous photos to gain likes.

o You have little time for self-care activities like eating, exercise, sleep, or self-reflection.

o Scrolling through social media leaves you feeling envious, depressed, anxious, or angry.

o Your symptoms of anxiety, depression, or loneliness are increasing.

If you checked any of the above, it's time to reassess your social media habits. Consider reducing the time you spend on it or possibly even step away from it for a short period of time in order to safeguard your mental health.

• Number a piece of paper from one to twenty-one. Then return to the list of traits found in healthy relationships. As you think about the adults in the family you grew up, use the following scale to rate the degree to which they displayed each trait. Then do the same for your significant other and any relationship you have with someone you consider to be a close friend. Finally, rate how well you display each trait.

Never = 0
Rarely = 1
Sometimes = 2
Often = 3
Always = 4

Do you see any patterns? Often, areas where your family was weak are reflected in both yourself and your current relationships. However, it's also common to seek and form relationships with people who are strong in areas where your family was weak.

- Select one trait that you scored yourself low on and create a summary sheet for it. When creating a summary sheet for a negative behavior you want to reduce, keep in mind the behavioral principle that the best way to reduce a negative behavior is to practice the opposite positive behavior. For example, if you tend to be critical, practice being encouraging. While you will probably revert to old habits when you are sick, hungry, tired, or stressed, your new behavior will slowly become part of you most of the time.

Here are two examples of summary sheets. The first was created by Robert, who wanted to become more affectionate towards his wife and children. The second was created by Nova, who wanted to become more encouraging. Note that each only contains three sections as the focus is on replacing unwanted behaviors with new ones.

Expressing More Affection Towards My Wife and Children
Why This Became an Issue?

My parents were so broken that they were unable to give me the love I needed as a child. They were often cold and rejected me. While I developed rigid walls to protect myself, I still desperately wanted their love. I have been mirroring their behavior in my family.

Situations Where This Creates Problems

- I rarely say "I love you" when we make love.
- I often avoid holding my wife's hand when we're in public.
- I stiffen when someone hugs me. I rarely hug my children.
- I rarely say "I love you" to my children.
- I rarely express appreciation.

Things I Can Practice

- Tell my wife "I love you" during tender times when we're alone.
- Hold my wife's hand when we're in public.
- Give my wife a hug when she returns home and hug my children at least once a day.
- Allow others at church to hug me and hug them back.
- Tell my children "I love you" at least once a day.
- Practice expressing gratitude to others whenever they do something for me.
- I can read a book about love languages.

Become More Encouraging

Why This Became an Issue

Both my father and mother were perfectionists. They always stressed that if you do a job, you should do it well. They were critical and always seemed to find something about what I had done that fell short of their expectations. Now, I do this with my husband and children.

Situations Where This Creates Problems

- When my husband or children make a mistake, I always point it out.

- I constantly point out times when my husband forgets something, such as turning off a light.
- I rarely say anything to my husband or children when they do something well. If I say anything, I just say, "That's nice."
- I look for what's wrong in whatever situation I'm in.

Things I Can Practice

- I can remain silent when my husband catches himself doing something wrong or making a mistake.
- I can remain silent when my husband forgets something and just take care of it.
- I can encourage my husband and children by finding one specific thing I like when they do something.
- I can say "Thank you," when people do something nice for me.
- I can look for at least two positive things wherever I am.
- I can read about how to encourage others on the Internet.

Chapter 11:

Purpose and Meaning

Dig deep enough in every heart and you'll find it: a longing for meaning, a quest for purpose. As surely as a child breathes, he will someday wonder, "What is the purpose of my life?"

– Max Lucado

C hapter 10 identified positive relationships as being the most important contributor to a sense of subjective well-being, or what is commonly called happiness. In this chapter, we explore the next two key elements of happiness: purpose and meaning.

PURPOSE

Modern research by psychologists on the role of purpose in people's lives started with the experiences of Nazi concentration camps survivors. Viennese psychologist Viktor Frankl had been a prisoner at Theresienstadt, Auschwitz, and two satellite camps of Dachau. He noticed that fellow prisoners who had a sense of purpose showed greater resilience as they faced torture, slave labor, and starvation. His 1959 book,

Man's Search for Meaning, described what he had learned about the importance of meaning and purpose in people's lives.

A common mistake is to think of goals and purpose as being the same thing. One of the key differences is time. A goal is something that can be achieved at some fixed point in time. For example, "I want to get a degree in psychology." Purpose is the reason for achieving a goal and cannot be completed at a fixed point in time. Instead, it provides a direction and influences the setting of goals. For example, "I want to get the degree so I can help people live more meaningful lives." This purpose–helping people live more meaningful lives–drives the immediate goal of getting a degree. It will also guide the setting of future goals.

A strong correlation in studies done both in the U.S. and Asia has shown that those who had a strong connection to their sense of purpose lived longer than those who didn't. Studies have also shown an association between a lower level of purpose and heart disease, premature death, and Alzheimer's disease. For example, a study of almost 7,000 people, published in *Journal of the American Medical Association (JAMA) Network Open* concluded, "This study's results indicated that stronger purpose in life was associated with decreased mortality. Purposeful living may have health benefits."

Another study of retired employees of Shell Oil found that men and women who retired early (age 55) were more likely to die early than those who retired at age 65. A similar study of almost 17,000 healthy Greeks showed that the risk of death increased by 51% after retirement. Studies like these show the risk when one's sense of purpose and meaning are only found in a career. They also indicate that finding a new sense of purpose after retirement improves the chances of a longer, healthier life.

It's important to note that while studies like these show a strong association between a sense of purpose and health, they do not prove causation. Psychologist Anthony Burrow found that the benefits of purpose may come from the important role it plays in how we relate to the world around us. His research found that people with a strong sense of purpose aren't as emotionally affected when confronted by the ups and downs of life. "It's not the absence of stress, it's how we react to it," Burrow says. "That's potentially the explanatory mechanism that affects health. Purposeful people can mitigate stress that would otherwise derail them."

If you have a strong sense of purpose, good. However, if you currently do not have something that excites you when you get up, a good place to start is to explore your interests. Is there a particular subject you find intriguing when online or talking to others? Do you get excited when talking about politics, nature, or something you do at work or as a hobby? The things you like to talk about and the things you enjoy sharing on social media may reveal what can give you purpose in life. After you've identified what generates a fire inside of you, think about the skills, talents, and passions you bring to the table. Then brainstorm how you might turn your passion into something meaningful to you.

A purpose might come from something you do in your free time, such as a hobby, music, sports, or a church or charitable activity. It might even be something you found exciting when you were young, but abandoned when the demands of adult life pressed in on you. A sense of purpose that involves something larger than you is more engaging than something that only benefits you. So, think about societal needs or injustices that stir you. For example, someone with a heart for the elderly might find a service activity, such as providing meals or visiting shut-ins rewarding. Someone who enjoys nature might find an organization that restores local habitat meaningful. The possibilities are endless.

It also helps if your sense of purpose is related to the meaning discussed in the next section. When your purpose works in conjunction with a wider worldview, you feel you are part of something bigger than yourself. This helps energize you in working towards goals generated by your purpose.

While some have a single driving purpose throughout their lives, others find that their purpose changes as they go through the normal stages of life. A key purpose in one's twenties may change when they enter midlife. It may then change again in old age. It's also common to have more than one key purpose in life. For example, a person may find a deep sense of purpose from both family and career. Another may find purpose in both a hobby and work.

MEANING

Throughout history, one of the questions that humans have asked is, "What is the meaning of life?" We are all hungry for meaning, for the feeling that our life is worth more than the sum of its parts and that our life matters in some way.

Research has found that those who find meaning in life, enjoy many benefits. Australian psychologist Lisa Williams conducted a study with 7,304 participants 50 years and older. Over the course of two years, the lives of those with a higher sense of meaning in life enjoyed better health and well-being. They had:

- Lower risk of divorce
- Lower risk of living alone
- Increased connections with friends and engagement in social and cultural activities
- Lower incidence of new chronic disease and onset of depression
- Lower obesity and increased physical activity
- Increased adoption of positive health behaviors (exercising, eating fruit and vegetables).

In another study, a large multi-university team looked at 8,492 participants from 30 colleges and universities. It found that "respondents with profiles high on presence of meaning showed the most adaptive psychosocial functioning" while those who felt their lives lacked meaning showed opposite patterns, leaving them feeling depressed, anxious, and more likely to engage in acts of social and physical aggression.

While research like this shows the importance of meaning, there is still much discussion about how to define meaning, so it can be the subject of research. Another problem is that meaning and purpose are sometimes used interchangeably. However, while purpose provides reasons for choosing a goal, meaning is what helps you find purpose.

Meaning comes from your ability to make sense of and understand your inner self, the world around you, how you fit within the world, and whether you perceive your life to be significant and important in some way. When positive psychologists try to define meaning, they identify two core elements: coherence and significance.

Coherence refers to how well your beliefs are logically interconnected and allow you to make sense out of life. It's the ability of your beliefs to provide an explanation for why things happen that is personally satisfying. This doesn't mean that you can easily fit every new event neatly into your beliefs about yourself and the world, but you can usually make some sense of them afterwards.

Significance is the belief that your life matters. It has value and is important in some way. Finding coherence and significance involves answering questions such as:

- Who am I?
- Why am I here?
- What is truly important to me?
- What am I supposed to do with my life?

Finding answers to questions like these that are personally satisfying helps make life feel meaningful. Many find answers to questions like these within the context of family and work, such as being a good parent or being successful at work. However, when your ideas about meaning mainly come from relationships, activities, or material things, your sense of meaning, basic assumptions about life, and worldview can be violently shaken by negative experiences such as:

- The death of a loved one
- Divorce, separation, or another break in a relationship
- Loss of a job due to retiring, getting fired, or laid off
- Natural disaster like floods, fire, or earthquakes

- Becoming the victim of a serious crime
- Suffering a trauma because of participating in combat
- Near-death experiences
- Sustaining serious injuries
- Becoming disabled
- Getting diagnosed with cancer or a debilitating disease

A growing body of evidence suggests that a spiritual outlook can be a major asset in coping with trauma like this. Psychologist Donald Meichenbaum defines spirituality as "an attempt to seek meaning, purpose and a direction of life in relation to a higher power, universal spirit or God. Spirituality reflects a search for the sacred." These types of beliefs are also sometimes referred to as existential beliefs–beliefs about one's existence. Having an existential belief system that goes beyond just finding meaning in family or work has been shown to not only make people happier, but it also makes them more resilient to trauma.

There are probably several reasons for this. First, people with well-developed existential or spiritual beliefs have a greater sense of significance than those without. They see that they matter. They are also more likely to engage in activities that research has identified as promoting happiness:

- Expressing gratitude
- Performing acts of kindness
- Practicing meditation or prayer
- Practicing forgiveness
- Having close relationships due to being part of a supportive community

- Thinking of yourself less because of being more engaged with the world
- Moving beyond small talk with those you are close to and discussing things that are deeply personal and important to you

A spiritual or existential belief system that boosts happiness and makes you more resilient to the bumps and bruises in life can contain many different elements. Here are two common elements.

Origin

The first and most basic questions you need to answer are: "Where did the universe come from?" "Why does it exist?" "Is it the result of random events, or is there evidence of intelligent design that points to a power or reality beyond what we see?" While many don't realize it, your answers to these questions provide a foundation for all your other existential beliefs.

Death

When I die, do I simply turn to dust and disappear, or is there some part of me–a soul or spirit–that lives on? Your answer to this question plays a major role in your ability to come to terms with your mortality–the fact that someday your physical body will stop working. The fear of death is behind many of the anxieties and fears that plague people. Those who are at peace with their mortality experience less internal stress when dealing with life's many problems, especially those connected to health issues and losing loved ones.

Some who believe that death is the end of existence deal with it by refusing to think about death. This works until they encounter the death of people they love or face their own death. Others accept death as just another part of life. They have a philosophy similar to the Greek Stoic philosopher Epictetus, who said, "I cannot escape death, but at least I can escape the fear of it." For many, the thought of an afterlife offers comfort.

If you do not have existential or spiritual beliefs about death that offer comfort, you may find it helpful to read about near-death experiences that occur when people are clinically dead. They offer powerful evidence that death is not the end of life.

The scientific study of near-death experiences began after the publication of psychologist Raymond Moody's book, *Life after Life*, in 1975. Since then, there has been a wealth of research on the subject. For example, one extensive study involving 2,060 patients from 15 hospitals conducted in 2014 concluded:

- The themes relating to the experience of death appear far broader than what we have understood so far, or what we have described as so-called near-death experiences.

- In some cases of cardiac arrest, memories of visual awareness compatible with so-called out-of-body experiences may correspond with actual events.

- A higher proportion of people may have vivid death experiences, but do not recall them due to the effects of brain injury or sedative drugs on memory circuits.

- The recalled experience surrounding death merits a genuine investigation without prejudice.

People who reject the possibility of anything supernatural usually consider near-death experiences as hallucinatory or illusory in nature. However, as this and other studies show, this explanation just doesn't work. While describing one example from the study, Dr Parnia concluded: "It has often been assumed that experiences in relation to death are likely hallucinations or illusions, occurring either before the heart stops or after the heart has been successfully restarted, but not an experience corresponding with 'real' events when the heart isn't beating. In this case, consciousness and awareness appeared to occur during a three-minute period when there was no heartbeat. This is paradoxical, since the brain typically ceases functioning within 20-30 seconds of the heart stopping and doesn't resume again until the heart has been restarted. Furthermore, the detailed recollections of visual awareness in this case were consistent with verified events."

Currently, the largest organization dedicated to near-death experiences is the International Association of Near-Death Studies that was founded in 1981. It has compiled thousands of reports on near-death experiences, along with numerous studies and articles for lay readers.

In a recent interview, Dr. Moody stated that after talking with over a 1,000 people who have had these experiences, he is confident that there is a life after death. One important feature of this type of research is that near-death experiences demonstrate that there is more to reality than the physical world we live in. If, after looking into this research, you also find this to be true, it can have a profound impact on your existential beliefs.

If you have thought little about the questions connected to origin and death—questions that the philosophers and religions of every culture have wrestled with–I encourage you to take time to clarify your beliefs about them. Since this is a very personal issue, it's hard to give specific guidelines. However, a good place for many to start is with existential or spiritual beliefs you grew up with. If you have thought little about them since childhood, take some time to explore them again as an adult.

If spiritual topics were rarely discussed when you were young, take some time to read a few books or watch a few videos that deal with each of the above two areas. You can also take time to attend a lecture or talk with someone active in a church or philosophy that you've been curious about.

The next chapter contains some closing thoughts.

SUMMARY OF KEY POINTS

- Modern research into the importance of purpose and meaning started with Viennese psychologist Viktor Frankl's 1959 book, *Man's Search for Meaning*.

- Goals and life purposes are different. A goal is something that is achieved at some fixed point in time. Purpose is the reason for achieving a goal and cannot be completed at a fixed point in time. Instead, it provides direction and influences the setting of goals.

- People with a strong sense of purpose live longer, experience better health, and greater resilience to stress.

- A purpose might come from many things such as family, free time interests, or something you found exciting when you were young.

- A sense of purpose that involves something larger than you is more engaging than something that only benefits you.

- One may have more than one key driving purpose in life.

- A key purpose at one stage of life may differ from one's purpose in another.

- Currently, positive psychologists researching the role of meaning in people's lives define it as having two components: coherence (why things happen) and significance (how I matter).

- Like purpose, meaning provides a host of relational, psychological, and health benefits.

- When your ideas about meaning mainly come from relationships, activities, or material things, negative experiences can violently shake your sense of meaning, basic assumptions about life, and worldview.

- Having an existential belief system that goes beyond just finding meaning in family, activities, or work helps not only make people happier, but it also makes them more resilient to trauma and loss.

- People with a deeper existential or spiritual belief system are more likely to engage in activities that research by positive psychologists has identified as promoting happiness.

- Two key areas to consider for a robust existential belief system are:
  o Origin: "Where did the universe come from?" "Why does it exist?" "Is it the result of random events, or is there evidence of intelligent design that points to a power or reality beyond what we see?"

o Death: "What happens when I die?"

- The study of thousands of near-death experiences provides strong evidence of life after death.

- Research into near-death experiences demonstrates that there is more to reality than the physical world we live in.

THINGS TO DO

- You can think of your purpose as a mission statement for your life. Create a short mission statement that describes your purpose in life. Here are several examples:

I want to:

o Help children be more than they thought they could be.

o Excel in my career and retire knowing that I have made exceptional contributions to my field of expertise.

o Be a leader who inspires his employees to be at their best.

o Help children who were abused become happy and successful adults.

o Bring joy to the world through music and lyrics that inspire.

o Help people who are struggling with disabilities.

o Bring more convenient and functional technology to the world that will improve people's quality of life.

o Use my cooking skills to bring families and individuals nutritious, tasty food options.

The chapter mentioned that many people have more than one key purpose in life. If this is the case for you, write two statements of purpose.

- The following questions were adapted from an article by Dr. Susan Krauss Whitbourne and published in *Psychology Today* and are based on the Meaning in Life Questionnaire developed by University of Minnesota-Twin Cities psychologist Michael Steger and colleagues (2006). They help you look at where your sense of meaning currently comes from, and identify areas where you might seek further development:

  o What about your life is meaningful? Something that is often suggested to help answer this question is to write your own epitaph. If you were to do so, would it have a clear purpose and sense of direction?

  o Can you clearly identify how your life is significant? You don't have to be famous or brilliant or have done something recognized by society to have significance. Believing your life has significance isn't the same as being significant in the public eye.

  o Do the things that you do and those that have happened in your life make sense to you?

  o Is the desire to have positive and meaningful relationships an important part of your life's purpose? While you can see your life as meaningful in its own right, those with a sense of purpose are usually part of a social network.

If you can give clear answers to each of the above, you probably have a strong sense of meaning in your life. For those areas where you are having difficulty in providing an obvious answer, think about what actions you could take to develop this area.

- Write a brief statement of your existential or spiritual beliefs concerning:

  o Origin: "Where did the universe come from?" "Why does it exist?" "Is it the result of random events, or is there evidence of intelligent design that points to a power or reality beyond what we see?"

  o Death: "What happens when I die?"

- If you do not have a well-thought-out set of existential or spiritual beliefs about the above that give you peace, spend some time researching online the ideas presented in this chapter. You might also find it helpful to talk to someone you know and trust about what they believe.

Chapter 12:

Continuing Your Growth

Instead of trying to mend me, I decided to enjoy me. Instead of trying to solve me, I decided to discover me. It was one of the best decisions of my life.

– S.C. Lourie

Now that you've reached the final chapter, you might be wondering, "What next?" This chapter provides the answer with a set of general guidelines for managing emotions you can use in the months ahead, along with suggestions for getting even more out of this book.

GENERAL GUIDELINES FOR STRONG EMOTIONS

The following guidelines are designed to help you hear more clearly the messages your emotions are giving you. These messages may be about needs that are being neglected or some action you need to take.

The guidelines are especially useful whenever you experience emotions that are overwhelming or puzzling, as well as when you respond to a situation in a way that you later regret. If the situation you are in allows it, use these steps to process your emotions while you are in the middle of experiencing them. When this is not possible because you need to focus on the events taking place around you, wait and go through them later when you are in a quiet place where you won't be disturbed.

What Am/Was I Feeling?

Clearly identify what emotion you experienced. Be sure to use words that describe true emotions as discussed in Chapter 9. If you are working with inappropriate behavior, identify what you were feeling just before you reacted. If this is difficult for you, take some time to review Chapter 8, which addresses how to do this in detail.

What Triggered This Emotion?

Chapter 2 describes how fear, anger, and sadness are a response to a perceived threat or loss. Here are questions you can ask yourself when you experience these:

Fear – What threat triggered my fear?

Anger – What threat triggered my anger?

Sadness – What was lost or missing that is important to me?

When you identify the threat or loss, decide if it was real or only a perceived threat or loss. You might also consider whether this is a secondary emotion as described in Chapter 8 where I described how I would cover my embarrassment with anger.

Was My Emotional Response Appropriate?

When answering this question, first decide if the response was a logical response. For example, if there was a genuine threat, then some level of anger or fear would be appropriate. If a loss occurred, sadness would be appropriate.

Next, ask yourself if the level of your emotion fits the situation. If the emotion was logical and at an appropriate level of intensity, go on to the next step. If your level of emotion was inappropriate or if there was no real threat or loss, ask yourself the following questions:

- Was this a conditioned emotional response as described in Chapter 3 (Ellie's holiday anxiety because of a difficult childhood)?
- Did my thinking involve any of the forms of distorted thinking described in Chapters 5 and 6 (all-or-nothing thinking, overgeneralizing, magnification, minimization, should/must thinking, and circular why questioning)?
- Did a negative core response pattern that I've identified play a role? Chapters 4 through 8 identify several, such as a low sense of self-efficacy and the need to always be strong and never show weakness.
- Were there any hidden needs generating this emotion, such as the need for others to like me, the need to control others or events, the need to be right, or the desire for revenge?

Are the Actions I Took Appropriate?

Most of the time, simply asking yourself this question is enough. However, if you are not sure, talk to someone you trust who manages his or her emotions well and who has good judgment. An objective third person is often helpful in looking at your behavior more clearly.

Is There Some Further Action I Need to Take?

Strong emotions always indicate a need to take action. Sometimes the action involves dealing with unresolved hurts from the past, irrational beliefs, or negative core response patterns that are still active in your life. Sometimes the required action has to do with setting limits or confronting someone. Sometimes it involves making changes in your life or pursuing something your heart desires that you have been ignoring. Again, if you are having difficulty identifying what you need to do, an objective third party can often help.

TAKE A SECOND LOOK

If you read through this book like a novel, only looking for new information and doing few, if any, of the exercises, you've probably learned a few new things. However, you're probably still reacting to situations in the same way as when you started. The work done by the people you read about took place over many months and entailed much effort on their part. While it was hard, each of them was richly rewarded. If you have emotional responses you would like to change, I encourage you to work through the book again and take time to do the activities it describes.

If you did the activities while reading and found them useful, I encourage you to reread the book and do the activities a second time. It's impossible to get everything out of a book like this in one reading. Because the ideas and skills are interconnected and build on each other, understanding the information in the final chapters helps you understand the information in the beginning chapters in ways that were not possible when you first worked through them. Likewise, having some ability with the skills in the final chapters strengthens your ability to do those presented in the earlier chapters in a deeper and more life-changing manner.

As you go back through the material, spend extra time with those sections and exercises which you feel are especially important to you. If you read the book on your own, consider forming a small group to work through it. Many find that hearing others discuss the ideas that were presented greatly increases their understanding, and helps them apply them more effectively. Learning about the experience of others who have done the activities can also point to things you have missed.

A FINAL WORD

It is my hope that this book has given you new insights into your own emotions, along with ways to manage them more effectively. However, if you've struggled with difficult emotions for years, as hard as it may be, I encourage you to be patient. Chapter 3 discussed how your brain is not a computer, but an organic system made up of cells and connections that only change through a process of growth.

The healing of emotional wounds is never a direct path of constant improvement. Instead, it's a process of two steps forward and one step back. You *will* experience times when old patterns reemerge, and it seems like nothing has changed. These will probably occur when you're sick, hungry, tired, or facing unusual stress.

When this happens, remind yourself that the storm will eventually pass, and the progress you've made will once again be evident. So, while it may take time, if you continue to apply the ideas and tools in this book to your life, they will work.

I thank you for the chance to enter into your life
through this book.

Appendix 1:

Suggestions for Selecting a Therapist

When seeking therapy, remember that a given therapist does not work effectively with every type of person or problem. It's important to find someone with both the skills and personality that are a good fit with you and the issue you wish to address. If possible, find someone who is licensed. While licensing does not guarantee competence, it does indicate that the state's standards of education and training have been met. Licensing can vary from state to state and country to country. However, my state, California, is representative of the four main types of licensed therapists:

Psychiatrists
These are medical doctors (M.D.) who, after their basic training in medicine, specialized in psychiatry. Their main focus is often on medication.

Psychologists
These usually have a doctorate (Ph.D.) in psychology. While many do general counseling, their focus is often on more severe types of mental disorders or psychological testing.

Marriage and family therapists

These usually have a master's degree (M.A. or M.S.), or sometimes a doctorate (Ph.D.), in counseling or psychology. They often focus on more common problems, such as family or relational issues or, like myself, problems with stress and anxiety or issues relating to a difficult childhood.

Social workers

They often work in social agencies. Social workers who conduct individual therapy are often referred to as clinical social workers. They usually have a master's degree (M.A. or M.S.), or sometimes a doctorate (Ph.D.), in social work.

If you know someone who has had therapy, they're often a good source for finding a therapist. You don't need to explain why you're asking. Just ask them to help point the way discreetly. You can also ask your physician for referrals, county mental health services, or seek a referral from a trusted clergy. You can also check to see if your medical insurance plan or work offers counseling. If none of these are available, you can do an Internet search. There are several ways you can do this. For example, if you are looking for a marriage and family therapist, type this along with the name of the city or area you live in.

marriage and family therapist in (your city or area)

You could also type the problem you wish to address along with your city or area.

panic disorder counseling in (your city or area)

If you live in an area where it is difficult to find a therapist who fits your needs, you might consider working with someone via the Internet.

After you have obtained the names of three therapists, give each a call. When calling, begin by describing as quickly and simply as possible your symptoms and any behaviors you want to eliminate or change. Many people find it helpful to have written notes to keep them focused. Next, ask the questions listed below. A good therapist welcomes questions about his or her treatment approaches and understands the importance of finding someone who matches your personality and problem. As you talk with each therapist, be sure to ask for an explanation whenever you do not understand what is being said. Two qualities you definitely want in your therapist are a willingness to answer questions directly and the ability to explain things clearly.

Are you licensed?

Since licensing varies from state to state, it's a good idea to ask what requirements need to be met for their license. Since some states do not issue licenses in all the above categories, you can also ask whether the therapist is a member of a professional association. If so, ask what requirements needed to be met in order to join the association.

How much experience or training have you had with my type of problem?

If at all possible, try to find someone who has experience dealing with the type of problem you are experiencing. If the therapist has little or no experience with your type of problem, it is best if he or she at least has some specific training that deals with it.

What is your basic approach to treatment?

This is probably the most confusing part of therapy, since there are many different terms used to describe therapeutic approaches. Fortunately, they all fall into the following three general categories:

PSYCHODYNAMIC

The focus in this approach is on finding patterns in your emotional responses, thoughts, and beliefs. These patterns are often traced back to childhood. The summary sheet section titled "Why This Became a Problem," along with the exploration of the core response patterns in Chapter 4, are typical of a psychodynamic approach.

COGNITIVE

This focuses on identifying irrational thoughts and beliefs that underlie dysfunctional behavior or difficult emotions. You then practice alternate ways of thinking. We can see this approach in the "Things I Can Tell Myself" section of the summary sheets, along with the presentation of the cognitive model in Chapter 2 and the distorted forms of thinking in Chapters 5 and 6.

BEHAVIORAL

This focuses on identifying specific times and places where a dysfunctional behavior occurs and practicing new behaviors that can replace dysfunctional ones. The "Situations Where This Creates Problems" and "Things I Can Do" sections of the summary sheets are what a behavioral approach focuses on.

Therapists often combine these approaches, as you have seen throughout the chapters of this book. Besides these general approaches, therapists might use a specific technique. An example would be eye movement desensitization and reprocessing (EMDR). With a skilled practitioner, this technique can be very useful in quieting emotional triggers associated with childhood abuse and adult trauma.

Does the standard course of treatment have a fixed length? If so, how long is it and are there provisions for follow up?
Some therapists do short-term therapy that lasts from eight to twenty weeks. Others prefer to do long-term therapy that can last a year or more.

How much does treatment cost and is any of it reimbursable by health insurance? What is your definition of success with my type of problem, and based on that definition, what is your rate of success?
Once you have chosen a therapist and have had two or three sessions, you will want to decide whether the therapist's personality and style seem right for you. It is best if you can answer most of the following questions with a yes.

Do I Feel
- That it's safe to say whatever I want when I am with the therapist?
- More hopeful and positive about myself at the end of most therapy sessions?
- That what the therapist says makes sense to me and seems relevant to my problems?

Did the Therapist Seem

- Comfortable with me?
- At ease rather than stiff and formal?
- Flexible and open to new ideas?
- Genuinely concerned about me?

During Our Sessions, Does the Therapist

- Take time to establish a set of goals for my therapy that I am able to understand; and is the therapist willing to use these goals to make periodic evaluations (every four to six weeks) of how the therapy is going and to set new goals, if it seems appropriate?
- Treat me with respect rather than as if I am sick, defective, or about to fall apart?
- Avoid acting as a superior and make me feel like an equal?
- Admit limitations rather than pretend to know things he or she does not know?
- Answer direct questions in a simple, straightforward manner?
- Find it easy to admit when he or she is wrong and apologize for making errors or for being inconsiderate?
- Welcome and encourage my viewpoint when I disagree rather than reacting negatively or telling me I am resisting?
- Allow me to direct the conversation if I want to do so?
- Act as if he or she is my consultant rather than the manager of my life?
- Show empathy and caring and give value to my feelings and thoughts?

- Reveal things about him or herself either spontaneously or in response to my questions and do this without bragging or monopolizing the conversation?

While it is important to find someone you are comfortable with, it is also important to remember that your goal is to quiet the emotional responses and behaviors that concern you. Do not allow therapy to drag on for months with no progress. While many problems do require long-term therapy, there is usually some sense of progress after four to six sessions. Of course, progress will be slower for a person from a dysfunctional family who experienced much physical, emotional, or sexual abuse than it will be for a person from a reasonably healthy family with only one or two issues that need to be addressed.

If you do not feel you have made any progress after six sessions, however, you might want to change therapists. Your time, money, and well-being are at stake. You are not obligated to a therapist simply because you started or have been with him or her for months or years. However, it is usually best to discuss this with your therapist before ending. This is also true when you feel you are ready to end therapy. Often, when a client feels they are ready to end regular sessions, a therapist will recommend a break followed by a "check-up" session to see how you are doing.

When you feel that you want to either end therapy or change therapists, it is usually best to discuss this with your current therapist before you take action. The only exception to this would be if the therapist makes sexual advances toward you or does anything else that is clearly unprofessional. If this ever occurs, leave immediately and report what has happened to your state licensing agency. If there is no licensing of therapists in your state, report the incident to the professional organization to which the therapist belongs.

If you have changed therapists several times and have tried several different approaches with little progress, it may be that you have not made a real commitment to the therapeutic process or failed to give any one approach enough time. If this is the case, you may find it beneficial to resume work with the therapist who seemed most effective and discuss your concern about a lack of progress.

Appendix 2:

Self-Help Groups

elf-help groups and short-term structured programs provide a valuable resource for people dealing with a variety of issues. If you're in therapy, these groups and programs can provide an excellent supplement or follow-up to professional treatment. You may also find them valuable if professional treatment is either not available or not affordable. Even people who do not feel their problems are severe enough to warrant professional treatment often find self-help groups a valuable resource.

Self-help groups are sometimes referred to as mutual-help or support groups. They deal with a wide variety of issues, such as anxiety, depression, physical disabilities, eating and food issues, addiction, bereavement, and illness. Groups like these are usually made up of individuals who share the same or a similar concern or issue. Members provide emotional support and advice to each other. Many are part of a national organization, such as Alcoholics Anonymous (AA). Some have a religious base, such as Celebrate Recovery. Other options may be sponsored by a local trained professional, hospital, or church.

Membership is usually free or involves only a minimal fee or donation. While a well-run self-help group can often be valuable, you do need to evaluate whether a particular group is helping or hurting you. A well-run group will have a set of ground rules. While these may vary depending on the type of group and who is running or sponsoring it, the following are usually included:

- Confidentiality is essential. What is said in the group is not to be repeated or discussed outside of the group.
- Members are encouraged to accept other participants just as they are and avoid making judgments.
- Everyone is given an opportunity to share.
- Members have the right to speak and the right to remain silent.
- Members are to avoid side conversations and give supportive attention to the person who is speaking.
- Members have the right to ask questions and the right to refuse to answer.
- The group does not discuss members who are not present.
- Meetings begin and end on time.

If a group feels toxic or abusive, leave.

A good place to start when looking for a local self-help group is online. Start your search with a few words that describe your problem, such as "anxiety" or "grief recovery". Add the name of the town or area you live in and the words "support", "self-help", or "self-help group". The quotation marks tell the search engine to look for that term first. For example:

"anxiety" self-help groups in Sacramento CA

"grief recovery" support group in Sacramento CA

Other places to look at are national organizations that deal with the issue you're facing. A few examples in the U.S. would be National Alliance on Mental Illness (NAMI), Depression and Bipolar Support Alliance (DBSA), Anxiety & Depression Association of America (ADAA), Alcoholics Anonymous (AA), and Al-Anon. They often have a listing of groups and therapists in various areas. Therapists who specialize in the issue you are dealing with may also know of a local group. Churches are yet another place where self-help groups often meet.

After you have the names of several possible groups, identify the one that seems best for you. If there are several groups in your area dealing with your issue, attend more than one to find the one that is best for you. Your goal is to find a group that matches your needs and personality.

About the Author

RENEAU Z. PEURIFOY spent his early years in San Diego, California, while his father served in the U.S. Navy. After the completion of his father's twenty-one-year naval career, Reneau was in the third grade, and the family moved to a home on a large parcel of land just outside of Sacramento, California. This became home to not only the family, but a large vegetable garden and numerous animals including: cats, dogs, a parrot, chickens, and rabbits.

Reneau graduated from California State University in Sacramento (CSUS) with a bachelor's degree in biology that included minors in chemistry and math. He met his wife, Michiyo, while attending CSUS. Together they raised two children, a boy and a girl.

After earning his degree at CSUS, Reneau completed studies for a secondary teaching credential. He then spent five years teaching science and math at both the junior high and high school levels. Two of those years were in Japan at St. Joseph College, a first through twelfth grade international school.

Upon his return to the United States, he pursued a master's degree in counseling at the University of San Francisco (USF). After graduation, he began an internship and was later licensed as a marriage and family therapist. He opened a private practice located in a suburb of Sacramento, where he specialized in working with anxiety disorders.

During the time that Reneau was in private practice, he was invited to speak at nine national conferences put on by the Anxiety Disorders Association of America (ADAA), the nation's primary organization for anxiety-related problems. He also conducted numerous local classes covering a wide range of topics, such as effective parenting and stress management. After twenty years, he retired from private practice to teach at a local college.

Reneau is now retired from teaching but continues to be active writing and speaking to various groups. In addition to *Why You Feel the Way You Do*, he is also the author of *Anxiety, Phobias, and Panic: Taking Charge and Conquering Fear, Overcoming Anxiety: From Short-Term Fixes to Long-Term Recovery*, and *Anger: Taming the Beast*.

He also has an active YouTube channel and posts regular articles at

www.whyemotions.com